GOLDEN KEYS TO ULTIMATE FAVOR

Divine Secrets for a Life Crowned
with Glory and Honor

DAVID S. PHILEMON

Royal Diadem Publishing INC

Book Title: GOLDEN KEYS TO ULTIMATE FAVOR
Author: DAVID S. PHILEMON
Phone Number: +1 773 521 3954
Email Address: info.royaldiadempublishing@gmail.com

This book was designed and published by:

Royal Diadem Publishing INC
 info.royaldiadempublishing@gmail.com
 +1 773 521 3954

All scripture quoted are taken from King James Version of the Bible

Dedication

*I dedicate this book, Golden Keys to Ultimate Favor, first and
foremost to the Lord Jesus Christ my source, my strength,
and the giver of every good and perfect gift. Without His
grace, none of this would be possible. To my beloved children,
spiritual children, and the precious members of Church on Fire
International you inspire me daily to press deeper into God's
purpose. Your faith, hunger for the Word, and testimonies
remind me that God's favor is alive and working in His people.
Finally, to every reader who holds this book in their hands
this is for you. May these golden keys unlock doors you never
dreamed possible, position you for divine encounters, and usher
you into a lifetime of supernatural favor.
With love and gratitude, Apostle Dr. David Philemon*

ACKNOWLEDGEMENT

This book would not have been possible without the unwavering support, dedication, and talent of an extraordinary team. My deepest gratitude goes to each of you for your contributions, insights, and encouragement throughout this journey.

First and foremost, thank you to Rev. Mimi Philemon, my dear wife; my brother-in-law, Rev. Shina Gentry; my Assistant Pastor, Rev. Bright Amudoaghan; and the Lead Pastor of Church on Fire International, Pastor Peculiar Onyekere, for your incredible effort, encouragement, and steadfast belief in this project. Your support has been instrumental in bringing this vision to life.

To the dedicated leaders of Royal Diadem Publishing, Ide Imogie and Kishawna Bailey, I am immensely grateful for believing in this project from the very beginning and for investing your time and energy into its development. Your creativity, dedication, and expertise have been the backbone of this endeavor.
I am especially thankful to the entire Royal Diadem Publishing team for your meticulous attention to detail, refining every page, and ensuring that each word reflects our shared vision.

A heartfelt thank you to my family, friends, and colleagues, whose unwavering encouragement and faith in this work gave me the courage and strength to see it through.

Finally, to all the readers and supporters who give meaning to these pages thank you. I am humbled and honored to share this journey with each of you.

With all my gratitude, David Philemon

Special Call To Salvation & New Beginnings From Apostle Dr. David Philemon

Dear Beloved, You are not reading this by accident God Himself has led you here because He loves you more than you could ever imagine. No matter where you've been, what you've done, or how far you feel from Him, His arms are open wide to receive you today.

The Bible says in John 3:16: "For God so loved the world that He gave His one and only Son, that whoever believes in Him shall not perish but have eternal life." That means you. Jesus Christ came to take away your sins, heal your heart, and give you a brand-new life one filled with peace, purpose, and hope.

Today, you can step into that new life. If you are ready to surrender to Him, pray this from your heart:

The Salvation Prayer Heavenly Father, I come to You in the name of Jesus. I confess that I am a sinner in need of Your mercy. I believe that Jesus Christ is Your Son, that He died on the cross for my sins, and that You raised Him from the dead. Today, I turn away from my old life and give You my whole heart. Jesus, come into my life. Be my Lord, my Savior, and my best friend. Wash me clean, fill me with Your Holy Spirit, and guide me into the life You created me to live. Thank You, Father, for loving me, forgiving me, and making me Yours. In Jesus' name, Amen.

Welcome to the Family of God! If you prayed that prayer with faith, congratulations! Your sins are forgiven, your name is written in the Book of Life, and heaven is celebrating you right now. This is the beginning of the greatest journey you will ever take and you are not alone.

Your Next Steps:

* Connect with a Bible-believing church: You were never meant

to walk this journey alone.

* Read God's Word daily: The Bible will show you who God is and who you are in Him.

* Pray often: Talk to God about everything. He delights in hearing your voice.

* Share your testimony: Let others know what God has done for you.

Your life will never be the same again. God's plans for you are greater than you can imagine so walk forward in faith, knowing He is with you every step of the way.

CONTENTS

INTRODUCTION

Unlocking Divine Favor

Favor is a mystery that transforms lives, lifts destinies, and breaks barriers. It is the invisible force that causes things to fall into place effortlessly. The Bible repeatedly shows us that the difference between ordinary and extraordinary is in favor. In the life of a believer, nothing is more critical than understanding and walking in God's favor. It is what separates those who struggle through life from those who thrive in every season.

But what is favor, and why does it matter so much? Favor is more than just being liked by people or having good things happen to you. Favor is a divine endorsement, supernatural assistance that gives you an advantage beyond what you could earn or achieve. When God's favor rests on you, doors that were once closed suddenly open, battles you did not think you could win are won with ease, and you are positioned in places of influence that seem far beyond your reach.

In my years of ministry, I have witnessed the power of favor firsthand. It is not something you can manipulate or earn through your efforts. Favor is a gift from God, released when you align yourself with His will and purpose. Favor carries with it the weight of responsibility because it is not just for personal gain; it is meant to advance God's kingdom on earth.

Throughout this book, we will examine the various keys to unlocking a lifetime of divine favor. Taking from scriptural examples and personal experiences, I will show you how to access favor in different dimensions, how to sustain it, and how to use it for God's glory. We will look at the lives of people like

Joseph, Esther, Mary, and Daniel, who were not only blessed with favor but also used that favor to change their generation.

This teaching will challenge you to step into deeper levels of faith, obedience, and surrender to God. High favor is available, but it comes at a price, it requires faithfulness, humility, and the willingness to partner with God even when it's uncomfortable. The keys to unlocking this favor are hidden in the principles we will uncover together.

Whether you are struggling to break through barriers in your life, seeking a greater purpose, or simply wanting to walk more closely with God, this book is for you. I pray that as you read, the Holy Spirit will open your eyes to the favor already set aside for you. The keys to ultimate favor are within your reach. Are you ready to unlock them?

CHAPTER ONE

THE DIMENSIONS
OF FAVOR

F avor is one of the most powerful keys to success in life. It is not just about being liked or receiving kindness; it is a divine force that opens doors, creates opportunities, and brings the supernatural into the natural. In the realm of God, nothing significant happens without favor. The Bible shows us that from the Old Testament to the New Testament, those who accomplished great things in life had one thing in common: divine favor. Whether it was Joseph, Esther, Mary, or Daniel, they accessed various dimensions of favor that enabled them to fulfill their God-given purposes.

Now, favor is not a static experience. It comes in levels, and not everyone operates at the same level of favor. Just as there are different levels of faith, there are also various levels of favor that we can access, depending on our walk with God and our readiness to partner with Him.

Understanding The Levels Of Favor

When we speak of favor, we must understand that it exists in dimensions or categories. One can move from no favor to low favor, from low to high favor, and even beyond that into extraordinary favor. These levels are not randomly accessed;

they are unlocked through specific actions, spiritual maturity, and alignment with God's will.

The first category is *"No Favor"*. This is when a person is devoid of any divine assistance or intervention. Life feels like an endless struggle, where even the simplest tasks require immense effort, and nothing seems to work. The Bible tells us in Proverbs 13:15 that,

> *"Good understanding gains favor, but the way of the unfaithful is hard."*

Those who lack favor experience life as a hard road constantly met with resistance and frustration.

Moving up from *"No favor"* is *"Low Favor"*. There is some level of divine intervention, but it is limited here. The person may experience occasional breakthroughs or moments of ease, but they are sporadic and cannot be sustained. This is where many believers find themselves. They have moments where they can sense God's hand in their life, but it is not consistent enough to create lasting impact or change. Low favor opens doors, but those doors may not lead to the fullness of what God has prepared.

Next is *"Just Favor"*. This is the kind of favor many people are content with. It allows them to survive, to get by, and to enjoy a relatively comfortable life. However, it lacks the extraordinary nature that transforms and elevates. Jesus demonstrated this when he healed the ten lepers. They received favor, but only one returned to give thanks, and he was the one who experienced a higher level of favor beyond healing, the restoration of wholeness (Luke 17:11-19).

Finally, there is *"High Favor"*. This is the dimension where the supernatural becomes the norm in a person's life. High favor is what we see in the lives of Joseph, Daniel, and Mary. When the angel Gabriel visited Mary, he declared,

> *"Rejoice, highly favored one, the Lord is with you; blessed are you among women!" Luke 1:28.*

Mary was not just favored, she was highly favored, and as a result, she carried the Messiah.

How To Recognize And Unlock Each Level Of Favor

Recognizing the dimension of favor you are operating in is crucial to understanding where you are spiritually and what you need to do to access more of God's favor. Each level of favor has its signs and characteristics, often requiring different actions or attitudes to unlock higher dimensions.

No Favor: The Hard Road

The most apparent sign of having no favor is a constant struggle. Nothing works, and life seems to be a series of closed doors. You work hard, but the results are minimal or non-existent. People in this category often feel like they are swimming against the tide. The lack of flavor is sometimes a result of disobedience, neglecting spiritual principles, or simply being disconnected from God's purpose.

The first step to move out of this level is alignment with God's will. Psalm 5:12 tells us,

> *"For You, O Lord, will bless the righteous; with favor You will surround him as with a shield."*

Righteousness attracts favor. Aligning your life with God's word, obeying His instructions, and seeking to walk in His ways will open the door for a favor to begin manifesting in your life.

Another key to breaking out of no favor is humility and prayer. James 4:6 reminds us,

"God resists the proud, but gives grace to the humble."
Humbling yourself before God and acknowledging your need for His help is the starting point for accessing favor. The prodigal son did this in Luke 15:21 when he said,

> *"Father, I have sinned against heaven and in your sight, and am no longer worthy to be called your son."*

His humility triggered a restoration of favor in his life.

Low Favor: The Inconsistent Breakthroughs

At this level, you may experience periodic breakthroughs, but nothing is sustained. You see moments of God's goodness, often followed by periods of struggle or stagnation. People in this category tend to rely on their efforts more than they should, resulting in temporary success but not long-lasting progress. A lack of consistency in spiritual practices, such as prayer, worship, and obedience often characterizes low favor.

To move beyond low favor, faithfulness is critical. Luke 16:10 says,

> *"He who is faithful in what is least is faithful also in much."*

God increases favor in the lives of those who prove themselves faithful with the little they have been given. If you want to experience more favor, you must show God you can be trusted with what He has already placed in your hands.

Additionally, gratitude unlocks more favor. In the story of the ten lepers (Luke 17:11-19), the one leper returned to thank Jesus and received a more significant measure of favor. While the others were healed, this man was made whole. Gratitude multiplies favor because it acknowledges God as the source, and God delights in those who give Him glory for His works. When you thank God for the little favor you experience, He opens more doors for you.

Just Favor: The Comfortable Life

This dimension of favor allows a person to live comfortably. They experience a measure of God's blessing in various areas of life, spiritually, financially, and relationally, but it is limited to what they need to get by. Just favor sustains life but does not elevate it. Many people are content to live at this level because it meets their basic needs. However, just favor is not the ultimate goal for believers. God desires to give us life in abundance, not just life at a comfortable level (John 10:10).

To unlock more favor and move beyond just favor, believers must stretch their faith and begin to believe in greater things. It is easy to become complacent when things are going well, but God calls us to grow and go deeper in our walk with Him. This requires stepping out of the comfort zone. For instance, Abraham experienced favor when he was called to leave his homeland, but his willingness to trust God beyond the familiar led him to become the father of nations. Obedience to divine instructions, especially when they challenge you to leave your comfort zone, is essential to unlocking more favor.

High Favor: The Supernatural Lifestyle

High favor is where the supernatural becomes natural. At this level, believers walk in the kind of favor that attracts miraculous breakthroughs, divine appointments, and uncommon blessings. High favor is what Joseph experienced in Egypt, rising from an enslaved person to the second-most powerful man in the nation. Daniel experienced this when he gained favor with kings and became a trusted advisor in foreign lands. It is what Mary experienced when she was chosen to carry the Messiah.

At this level, the favor of God flows so abundantly that everything you touch seems to prosper. Proverbs 3:3-4 instructs us to keep God's commandments close to our hearts: *"Let not mercy and truth forsake you... so find favor and high esteem in the sight of God and man."* This level of favor is not just about personal benefit; it allows a believer to impact nations, influence kingdoms, and shift spiritual atmospheres.

A deep commitment to prayer and intimacy with God is crucial to maintaining and increasing high favor. High favor is sustained by those who walk closely with the Lord. Psalm 25:14 says,

> *"The secret of the Lord is with those who fear Him, and He will show them His covenant."*

Those who dwell in intimacy with God are shown mysteries and secrets that position them for favor at unprecedented levels.

Biblical Examples Of The Dimensions Of Favor

Throughout the Bible, we find examples of individuals who operated in different favor dimensions. These stories give us insight into how favor works and how we can move from one level to another. Each figure encountered unique circumstances, yet favor was the common thread that allowed them to overcome adversity, rise to positions of influence, and fulfill their God-given purposes.

· Joseph: From No Favor to High Favor

Joseph's life is one of the clearest examples of how favor can transform a person's destiny. At the start of his journey, Joseph experienced the painful reality of no favor. His brothers despised him, and he was sold into slavery. Betrayal, false accusations, and imprisonment marked his life. Yet, despite these hardships, Joseph remained faithful to God. Genesis 39:2 says,

"The Lord was with Joseph, and he was a successful man."

Even in the worst conditions, Joseph's favor began to manifest.

Joseph's faithfulness in Potiphar's house and later in prison showed his ability to steward low favor well. Though he was enslaved and later a prisoner, he was put in charge of everything in Potiphar's household and later in the prison. This marked a shift in his favor, moving him from no favor to low favor. He gained respect and trust, though his circumstances were still difficult.

The turning point in Joseph's life came when he interpreted Pharaoh's dream. This act of obedience and divine insight unlocked high favor, leading him to a place of influence and authority. Genesis 41:40 records Pharaoh's words:

"You shall be over my house, and all my people shall be ruled according to your word; only in regard to the throne will I be greater than you."

Joseph moved from a place of hardship to a position where the entire nation of Egypt depended on his wisdom and leadership. His high favor allowed him not only to save Egypt from famine but also to reconcile with his family and preserve the lineage of

Israel.

Lessons From Joseph:

Faithfulness in the midst of adversity is key to unlocking higher levels of favor. Joseph's story reminds us that favor can work even in difficult situations, but we must stay faithful and trust God through the process.

• Esther: Positioned for High Favor

Esther's story is another remarkable example of high favor. When she was chosen as queen, she was not just any woman; she was specifically chosen because of her divine favor. Esther 2:17 says,

"The king loved Esther more than all the other women, and she obtained grace and favor in his sight more than all the virgins."

Esther had just a favor in the sense that she was living in the palace and enjoying the privileges of being queen. However, it was not until she risked her life to save her people that she accessed high favor.

When the Jewish people were facing annihilation, Esther's favor positioned her to intervene. Yet, this was no ordinary intervention. To approach the king without being summoned was a death sentence unless the king extended his scepter. Esther understood that the favor in her life had to be activated through bold action. Esther 4:16 records her words:

> *"And so I will go to the king, which is against the law; and if I perish, I perish!"*

Her willingness to risk her life unlocked a dimension of favor that saved an entire nation. The king not only extended his scepter, but he also gave her the power to overturn Haman's wicked decree.

Lessons from Esther:
High favor often requires boldness and the willingness to step out in faith. Esther's courage and trust in God moved her from enjoying personal favor to impacting her entire generation.

• Mary: Chosen for the Ultimate Favor
The angel Gabriel's words to Mary in Luke 1:28,

"Rejoice, highly favored one, the Lord is with you,"

indicate that she was operating in a dimension of favor that few had ever experienced. Mary was chosen to carry the Son of God, a role that required the highest level of divine favor. Her favor was not just for personal blessing; it was a favor that would change the world.

Mary's story shows us that high favor often comes with great responsibility. She had to endure the social stigma of being pregnant before marriage, and she had to trust God in the midst of circumstances she could not fully understand. Still, her willingness to say,

> *"Behold the maidservant of the Lord! Let it be to me according to your word" (Luke 1:38),*

demonstrating the heart posture needed to sustain high favor.

Lessons from Mary:
High favor requires surrender to God's will, even when it comes with challenges. Mary's willingness to embrace God's plan, despite the difficulties, positioned her to be part of the greatest story ever told.

• Daniel: Favor in Foreign Lands
Daniel's life is a good example of how favor can elevate a person in hostile environments. Taken into captivity as a young man,

Daniel was placed in a foreign land under a pagan king. Yet, Daniel's commitment to God set him apart. Daniel 1:9 says,

"Now God had brought Daniel into the favor and goodwill of the chief of the eunuchs."

This low favor placed Daniel in a position of influence even though he was a captive.

Daniel's integrity and devotion to God, demonstrated by his refusal to defile himself with the king's food, unlocked high favor. He was later promoted to a position of great authority under King Nebuchadnezzar and continued to serve under multiple kings, each recognizing his exceptional wisdom and divine insight. Daniel 6:3 says,

"Then this Daniel distinguished himself above the governors and satraps because an excellent spirit was in him; and the king gave thought to setting him over the whole realm."

Lessons from Daniel

Integrity and faithfulness, even in difficult or hostile environments, attract high favor. Daniel's consistent devotion to God, regardless of the circumstances, allowed him to operate in high favor throughout his life.

Positioning Yourself For High Favor

From the stories of Joseph, Esther, Mary, and Daniel, we learn that accessing and walking in high favor is not an accident. It requires intentional positioning, spiritual maturity, and a willingness to partner with God's plans, even when they are challenging. High favor is the result of a divine relationship where trust, obedience, and faithfulness are key.

So, how can we position ourselves to access and operate in the highest levels of favor?

Develop A Lifestyle Of Faithfulness

As we saw in the life of Joseph, faithfulness in small tasks prepares us for greater opportunities of favor. Luke 16:10 says,

> *"He who is faithful in what is least is faithful also in much."*

God does not release high favor on people who have not proven themselves faithful in their current assignments. Whether it is in your workplace, family, ministry, or personal life, demonstrating integrity and faithfulness attracts the favor of God.

Faithfulness is not about waiting for a big break; it's about diligently doing the work in front of you. Joseph managed Potiphar's house with excellence and was later entrusted with managing an entire nation. Daniel stayed faithful to God's laws even when it could have cost him his life, and as a result, he was given favor in the courts of kings. Faithfulness creates a pathway for divine favor to manifest in ways we cannot imagine.

Pursue Intimacy With God

High favor is not just about external blessings; it is deeply tied to your relationship with God. Proverbs 3:3-4 tells us,

> *"Let not mercy and truth forsake you; bind them around your neck, write them on the tablet of your heart, and so find favor and high esteem in the sight of God and man."*

Mercy and truth come from walking closely with the Lord and aligning your heart with His. Those who walk in high favor are often those who prioritize intimacy with God above everything else.

Mary's high favor came because of her pure heart and willingness to trust God with the impossible. Esther's high favor was unlocked when she chose to fast and pray before approaching the king, showing her dependence on God. To access and sustain high favor, we must be people of prayer, worship, and devotion. When we seek God's heart, His favor naturally flows into our lives.

Practice Boldness and Obedience

High favor often requires taking bold steps of faith. Just as Esther boldly approached the king, knowing it could cost her life, we must be willing to take risks when God calls us. Favor is often unlocked when we step outside our comfort zones and obey God, even when the path ahead seems uncertain. Bold obedience positions us to receive favor that can influence nations, shift atmospheres, and transform lives. James 2:17 tells us that,

"faith by itself, if it does not have works, is dead."

Faith and boldness go hand in hand. When you believe that God has favored you, it will show in the way you act, make decisions, and take steps in life. Esther could have stayed quiet, but she recognized that her favor was for a greater purpose. High favor often brings us to pivotal moments where our obedience can change the course of history.

Be Humble and Grateful

Humility and gratitude are two of the most important qualities in attracting and sustaining favor. James 4:6 reminds us that

"God resists the proud but gives grace to the humble."

Those who walk in high favor do not see themselves as entitled to it. They recognize that favor is a gift from God, not something they earned by their own efforts. This is why Joseph, despite rising to great power, remained humble and gave credit to God for his success (Genesis 41:16).

Gratitude is another key to unlocking more favor. Just as the leper who returned to thank Jesus was made whole, showing gratitude for the favor you have already received will cause God to open new doors of opportunity. When we thank God for what He has done, we acknowledge that He is the source of every good thing in our lives, and we position ourselves for greater blessings.

Align with God's Purpose
Finally, high favor is reserved for those who align their lives with God's greater purposes. Favor is not just for personal benefit; it is meant to advance God's kingdom on earth. Esther, Joseph, Mary, and Daniel all operated in high favor because their lives were in alignment with God's plans for their generation. They understood that their favor was not just for their own comfort or success but for the salvation and deliverance of others. Isaiah 66:2 says,

"But on this one will I look: on him who is poor and of a contrite spirit, and who trembles at My word."

Those who tremble at God's word, meaning they take His instructions seriously and live according to His will, are the ones who experience the highest levels of favor. When you make God's mission your mission, He will release favor in every area of your life to ensure that His plans are accomplished through you.

Favor is a powerful key that can open doors no man can shut. It elevates, protects, and positions you for God's best in every area of your life. However, favor comes in dimensions, and to move from one level to another requires intentional action.

Faithfulness, intimacy with God, bold obedience, humility, and alignment with God's purpose are the keys to unlocking and sustaining high favor.

Just as Joseph, Esther, Mary, and Daniel accessed supernatural levels of favor by walking closely with God and obeying His instructions, we too can position ourselves for high favor. The path to high favor is one of trust, surrender, and courage. When we walk this path, God's favor will surround us, elevate us, and empower us to fulfill our destiny.

CHAPTER TWO

FAVOR AND DIVINE ASSIGNMENT

Favor is not random, nor is it given without purpose. When God grants favor, it is always tied to a divine assignment, that is, an opportunity to fulfill His will and bring glory to His name. Divine favor positions you to carry out tasks that are beyond your natural abilities and resources. It equips you for assignments that will have a lasting impact on the lives of others and the advancement of God's kingdom. Favor is God's way of empowering His chosen vessels to carry out His plans on earth.

From Genesis to Revelation, we see that those who walked in divine favor were entrusted with significant assignments. Their favor was not just for personal enjoyment or status; it was directly connected to their calling. Whether it was Joseph's rise to power in Egypt, Esther's intervention to save the Jewish people, or Mary's role in bringing the Messiah into the world, favor always came with a divine mission.

We will examine the relationship between favor and divine assignment, how God uses favor to accomplish His will, and what it takes to walk in alignment with your God-given purpose.

Favor Aligns With Purpose

God's favor is never wasted; it is always purposeful. When He releases favor, it is to equip you to fulfill the specific purpose He has called you to. This is why understanding your divine assignment is so important. Without a clear sense of purpose, you may not recognize the opportunities that favor brings your way.

In the story of Joseph, we see a powerful example of how favor aligns with divine purpose. Joseph's journey began with a dream, a vision from God that foretold his future role as a leader. However, before the fulfilment of that vision, Joseph faced years of hardship, betrayal by his brothers, slavery, and imprisonment. Still, even in these difficult circumstances, God's favor was at work. Genesis 39:21 says,

> *"But the Lord was with Joseph and showed him mercy, and He gave him favor in the sight of the keeper of the prison."*

God's favor was not just about making Joseph's life easier; it was about positioning him for his divine assignment. Each step of Joseph's journey was a preparation for the moment when he would rise to power in Egypt and save many lives during the famine. Had Joseph not remained faithful during his trials, he might have missed the opportunities that favor brought his way.

This teaches us an important lesson: Favor is often disguised as challenges. Joseph's hardships were the very things that positioned him for his divine assignment. If you are going through a difficult season, it may be that God is using it to prepare you for greater favor and a higher calling.

The Responsibility Of Favor

Walking in divine favor comes with responsibility. Favor is not just a gift to be enjoyed; it is a tool to be used for God's purposes. When God grants you favor, He expects you to use it to advance His kingdom, help others, and fulfill your divine assignment. This is why it is so important to understand that favor is tied to God's will, not just your personal desires.

Take the story of Esther, for example. Esther enjoyed the favor of the king, living a comfortable life as queen. But when the Jewish people were threatened with annihilation, her cousin Mordecai reminded her that her favor was not just for her own benefit. He said,

"Who knows whether you have come to the kingdom for such a time as this?" (Esther 4:14).

Esther realized that her favor was tied to a greater purpose, the salvation of her people. She could have chosen to remain silent, but she understood that favor comes with a responsibility. By risking her life to approach the king without being summoned, she used her favor to fulfill God's plan and deliver the Jewish nation.

This teaches us that favor is not just about blessings; it is about assignment. God does not grant favor for self-promotion or personal comfort. When He grants favor, it is because there is work to be done, work that will advance His kingdom and impact lives. As believers, we must be willing to accept the responsibility that comes with favor and use it to fulfill God's divine purposes.

Favour Equips You For Tasks

In the life of Esther, we see how favor opened an opportunity to save an entire nation. While living in the palace and enjoying her royal position, Esther could have remained comfortable, disconnected from the crisis facing her people. But when Mordecai alerted her to the threat against the Jews, Esther understood that her favor as queen was not coincidental. She realized that her position in the palace was a divine opportunity to fulfill a greater purpose. In Esther 4:14, Mordecai's words reminded her of this,

"For if you remain completely silent at this time, relief and deliverance will arise for the Jews from another place, but you and your father's house will perish. Yet who knows whether you have come to the kingdom for such a time as this?"

Esther seized the opportunity that her favor had provided. Instead of retreating in fear, she boldly approached the king and interceded for her people, knowing that she might lose her life. This moment of action not only saved the Jewish nation but also secured her legacy as one of the most influential figures in biblical history. Divine opportunities come with divine timing, and favor equips you to recognize and respond to those opportunities when they arise.

How To Recognize Divine Opportunities

- **Be Sensitive to God's Timing**: Divine opportunities often align with critical moments in your life or the lives of others. Esther's favor was linked to the right time, the moment her people needed deliverance. Favor often comes with a sense of urgency and purpose, so it is essential to remain sensitive to God's timing. Pray for discernment, as opportunities for favor are sometimes time-sensitive and must be acted upon immediately.

- **Stay Aligned with God's Purpose**: When you are in alignment with God's will, you are more likely to recognize the opportunities favor presents. If Esther had not been in tune with the needs of her people and God's plan, she could have missed her moment of destiny. Staying aligned with God's purpose keeps you in a position to recognize divine opportunities when they appear.

- **Be Willing to Take Risks**: Divine opportunities often require a leap of faith. Esther's decision to approach the king without being summoned was a significant risk, but her favor gave her the courage to take bold action. When God presents an opportunity, do not be afraid to step out in faith, trusting that His favor will carry you through.

Favor's Impact On Generations

One of the most powerful aspects of divine favor is its ability to transcend one's own life and impact future generations. Favor is not just for the immediate moment, as it can create a legacy that continues to bless others long after one is gone. This is why stewarding favor well is so important. How you handle the favor in your life can either release blessings or withhold them from those who come after you.

Generational Blessings Through Obedience

Abraham is one of the clearest examples of how favor can impact generations. God's favor on Abraham was not just for him but for his descendants. In Genesis 12:2-3, God promises Abraham,

> *"I will make you a great nation; I will bless you and make your name great; and you shall be a blessing... and in you all the families of the earth shall be blessed."*

Abraham's obedience to God, even when it requires great sacrifice, unlocked a generational blessing that extended through Isaac, Jacob, and ultimately to the entire nation of Israel.

Abraham's willingness to follow God's call, even when it meant leaving his homeland and offering his son Isaac as a sacrifice, set the stage for the favor of God to rest on his descendants. The Bible repeatedly refers to the God of *"Abraham, Isaac, and Jacob"* because Abraham's obedience created a ripple effect of favor that impacted multiple generations.

This teaches us that how we handle divine favor affects not only us but also those who come after us. When we align ourselves with God's purposes and steward favor with integrity, we create a legacy of blessing that can be passed down through our family line. Just as Abraham's favor brought blessing to his descendants, the favor on your life can position your children and future generations for success and divine favor.

The Multigenerational Reach Of Favor

Favor is not limited to your personal success or achievements, it has the power to affect communities, nations, and future generations. This is why it is important to view favor as something greater than yourself. When Joseph rose to power in Egypt, his favor did more than just elevate him to a position of influence. It provided a way for his entire family to survive the famine and flourish in a foreign land. In Genesis 50:20, Joseph reflects on how God used his favor not just for his own benefit but for the good of many,

> *"But as for you, you meant evil against me; but God meant it for good, in order to bring it about as it is this day, to save many people alive."*

Joseph's favor extended beyond his personal success to bring life and prosperity to the people of Egypt and his family. Similarly, the favor that God places on your life is meant to bless others, even those you may never meet. Your obedience and stewardship of favor can create opportunities, open doors, and provide resources for others to walk in their own divine assignments.

Leaving A Legacy Of Favor

Favor is an inheritance that can be passed down to future generations. The Bible is full of stories where favor was passed down from one generation to the next, from Abraham to Isaac to Jacob, from David to Solomon, and from the lineage of Jesus Christ Himself. The key to leaving a legacy of favor is to walk in obedience, steward favor with humility, and align your life with God's purposes. Psalm 112:1-2 says,

> *"Blessed is the man who fears the Lord, who delights greatly in His commandments. His descendants will be mighty on earth; the generation of the upright will be blessed."*

The favor on your life has the potential to leave a spiritual inheritance that will bless your descendants and those around you. When you walk in favor, you are not just creating a better life for yourself, you are laying the foundation for future generations to walk in the same favor and blessings.

Favor is not a random gift; it is deeply connected to your divine assignment. God grants favor to equip you, protect you, and provide for you as you carry out His will. But favor also comes with responsibility. It requires faithfulness, humility, and obedience to steward it well.

As you walk in divine favor, remember that it is not just for your benefit but for the advancement of God's kingdom and the blessing of others. Whether it is through recognizing divine opportunities, using your influence for God's purposes, or leaving a legacy of favor for future generations, your assignment is greater than yourself. By embracing the responsibility of favor, you can impact the world around you and create a lasting legacy that will continue to bear fruit for generations to come.

CHAPTER THREE

THE COST OF
HIGH FAVOR

Favor is a powerful and coveted blessing that can transform lives and circumstances. However, it is crucial to understand that high favor comes at a cost. Those who walk in divine favor often pay a price in terms of their comfort, obedience, and personal ambitions. High favor is a gift from God that positions individuals to fulfill their divine assignments, but it also demands a willingness to embrace sacrifice and commitment.

How Favor Aligns With Your Purpose

Favor is intrinsically linked to your God-given purpose. When God grants you favor, He is positioning you to fulfill the specific assignments He has for your life. Favor acts as a divine endorsement, enabling you to operate in your purpose with ease and effectiveness. It is essential to recognize that favor is not randomly distributed, it is given to those who are aligned with God's will and ready to carry out His plans.

Recognizing Your Divine Purpose

Understanding your divine purpose is the first step in accessing favor. God has a unique plan for each of us, and favor is His way of equipping us to fulfill that plan. The Bible is filled with examples of individuals who received favor because they were aligned with God's purpose.

For instance, in the life of Moses, we see how favor was connected to his calling to lead the Israelites out of Egypt. God chose Moses not only because of his lineage but also because of the specific purpose He had for him. When God appeared to Moses in the burning bush, He outlined the mission ahead and assured Moses of His favor,

"I will be with you" (Exodus 3:12).

Moses' purpose was to deliver his people, and God's favor was crucial in enabling him to accomplish that task. Favor granted Moses the authority to confront Pharaoh and perform miracles that demonstrated God's power.

Favor As Empowerment For Purpose

When you are aligned with your purpose, favor empowers you to achieve what you could not do on your own. The favor you receive is a reflection of your obedience to God's call. When you commit to following His plan, you can expect to experience divine favor that enhances your effectiveness in fulfilling your purpose.

Mary, the mother of Jesus, is another prime example of how favor aligns with purpose. When the angel Gabriel visited her, he proclaimed,

"Rejoice, highly favored one, the Lord is with you; blessed are you among women!" (Luke 1:28).

Mary's divine assignment was to carry the Messiah, and the favor she received was a testament to her alignment with God's will.

Mary's purpose requires great sacrifice and obedience, as she faced potential ostracism and hardship. However, her willingness to say,
"Behold the maidservant of the Lord! Let it be to me according to your word" (Luke 1:38),

positioned her to walk in high favor. God's favor empowered her to fulfill a purpose that would change the course of history.

The Role Of Favor In Fulfilling Divine Assignments

Favor is a critical factor in fulfilling divine assignments. When God calls you to a specific task, He provides favor as a means of support and empowerment. This favor can manifest in various ways, such as divine connections, resources, and opportunities that align with your calling.

• **Favor Creates Divine Connections:**
One of the ways favors facilitate divine assignments is through the creation of strategic connections. When you are walking in God's purpose, favor often brings the right people into your life at the right time. These connections can provide mentorship, guidance, and support that are essential for your journey.

For instance, consider the story of Esther. Esther's favor with King Xerxes positioned her to save her people from destruction. Her connection to the king was not mere coincidence; it was a divinely orchestrated relationship that allowed her to fulfill her assignment. When Mordecai urged Esther to intercede for the Jews, she understood that her favor as queen was a critical tool for saving her people (Esther 4:14). The opportunity to speak to the king could only have come through the favor that God had placed on her life.

Similarly, in the New Testament, we see how favor brought the early church together. The apostles experienced favor in the eyes of the people, leading to an explosion of growth and impact (Acts 2:47). These divine connections and relationships were essential for the expansion of the church and the fulfillment of the Great Commission.

- **Favor Provides Resources for the Assignment:**

Favor also plays a pivotal role in providing the resources needed to carry out God's assignments. When God calls you to a task, He equips you with everything necessary to succeed, often through favor that brings unexpected resources into your life.

In Nehemiah's story, when he was called to rebuild the walls of Jerusalem, he prayed for favor before approaching King Artaxerxes. As a result, the king not only granted Nehemiah permission to go but also provided him with letters for safe passage and timber for the construction (Nehemiah 2:8). This divine favor ensured that Nehemiah had the necessary resources to fulfill his mission.

God's provision through favor is not limited to material resources, it can also include spiritual insights, wisdom, and divine strategy. When you align your life with God's purpose, you can expect Him to provide everything you need to complete your assignment. This principle is echoed in Philippians 4:19,

> *"And my God shall supply all your needs according to His riches in glory by Christ Jesus."*

The Price Of Partnering With God For Favor

Partnering with God for high favor is not without its costs. While favor brings blessings and opportunities, it also demands that we live in obedience to God's will and embrace the sacrifices that come with fulfilling our assignments.

- **Sacrifice of Personal Ambitions**: One of the most significant costs of partnering with God for favor is the sacrifice of personal ambitions. When God calls you to a divine assignment, it often requires you to lay aside your own plans and desires in order to follow His purpose. This can be a difficult transition, especially if your ambitions are deeply rooted in your identity or sense of worth. Mary's acceptance of her role as the mother of Jesus is a profound example of this sacrifice. By agreeing to bear the Messiah, she put her own dreams and aspirations on hold. The social stigma, potential rejection, and the burden of raising the Son of God were heavy costs to bear. But then, Mary's willingness to submit to God's plan exemplifies the kind of sacrifice needed to partner with God for favor.

- **Commitment to God's Will**: High favor demands a commitment to God's will above our own. This means making choices that may not always align with our comfort or understanding. Following God's lead often requires stepping into the unknown and trusting Him for the outcome. The life of Abraham illustrates this beautifully. When God called Abraham to leave his homeland and venture into an unfamiliar land, He was asking Abraham to leave behind everything he knew. In Genesis 12:1, God said,

"Get out of your country, from your family and from your father's house, to a land that I will show you."

This call requires immense faith and commitment, but the favor that followed Abraham, becoming the father of nations, was worth the sacrifice.

- **The Challenge of Perseverance**: Lastly, partnering with God for high favor requires perseverance. The path to fulfilling divine assignments is often filled with challenges, setbacks, and moments of doubt. Maintaining your commitment to God's purpose during these times is crucial for experiencing the fullness of His favor. Consider the life of Joseph once more. After receiving favor from his father and being given prophetic dreams, Joseph faced betrayal, slavery, and imprisonment. His journey was fraught with trials, yet he remained faithful to God through it all. Joseph's perseverance ultimately led him to a place of high favor in Egypt, where he could fulfill his divine assignment of saving many lives during a time of famine (Genesis 50:20).

Sustaining Favor Through Faithfulness and Humility
Once we experience high favor, it is essential to maintain it through faithfulness and humility. The journey does not end with the attainment of favor; it requires continued dedication to God's purpose and a heart posture that reflects His character.

- **Faithfulness in Small Things:** Sustaining favor requires being faithful in the small things. Luke 16:10 tells us,

"He who is faithful in what is least is faithful also in much."

When you are entrusted with favor, God expects you to manage it wisely and faithfully. This means honoring God in every aspect of your life, whether in your work, relationships, or ministry. Faithfulness develops a reputation of reliability and integrity, attracting more favor. Just as Joseph demonstrated faithfulness in Potiphar's house and in prison, we too must be diligent in fulfilling our responsibilities. God's favor is attracted to those who prove themselves faithful, even in the mundane tasks of life.

- **The Importance of Humility:** Humility is another critical factor in sustaining favor. When we experience God's blessings, it is easy to become proud or complacent. However, Scripture warns us that

"God resists the proud, but gives grace to the humble"
James 4:6.

To maintain high favor, we must remain humble, recognizing that all we have comes from God. David, despite his rise to king, exemplified humility throughout his life. He understood that his favor was a gift from God and not a result of his own efforts. When David sinned and was confronted by Nathan the prophet, he did not make excuses, instead, he repented wholeheartedly. This humility allowed him to regain God's favor and continue fulfilling his purpose as king.

High favor is a precious gift that comes with a cost. It requires obedience, integrity, sacrifice of personal ambitions, and a commitment to God's will. Favor aligns with your purpose, empowering you to fulfill divine assignments and create a legacy of blessing for future generations.

As you go through the journey of walking in high favor, remember that while the cost may be high, the rewards are immeasurable. The opportunity to impact lives, fulfill God's purposes, and experience His blessings is worth every sacrifice. Embrace the cost of high favor, and watch as God unfolds His plans in and through your life.

CHAPTER FOUR

FAVOR IN ADVERSITY

◆ ◆ ◆

How Favor Manifests During Trials

Adversity is a common experience in life, and for many, it can feel overwhelming and isolating. However, the beautiful truth for believers is that God's favor often shines the brightest during our darkest moments. While trials can be painful, they are also opportunities for God's favor to manifest in ways that we may not expect.

Favor during adversity does not mean the absence of struggle, rather, it is the presence of God's grace and support that allows us to navigate through challenges with hope, strength, and purpose. When faced with trials, God's favor can provide comfort, direction, and even miraculous breakthroughs that demonstrate His power.

The Example Of Job

The story of Job is one of the most perfect illustrations of how favor can manifest in adversity. Job was a man who had everything: wealth, family, and a close relationship with God. However, in a series of devastating events, he lost it all, his wealth, his children, and his health. Despite his suffering, Job remained faithful to God, declaring,

"Though He slay me, yet will I trust Him" (Job 13:15).

Job's unwavering faithfulness in the face of adversity is a testament to the power of God's favor. Even in his lowest moments, Job experienced God's presence and favor in profound ways. Although he endured immense pain, God ultimately restored Job's fortunes, giving him twice as much as he had before (Job 42:10). This restoration was not just a return to what Job lost, it was a manifestation of God's favor, demonstrating that adversity does not equate to abandonment.

Through Job's story, we learn that favor often manifests in our trials by providing us with the strength to endure. Job had moments of despair and questioning, but he consistently turned to God in prayer and worship. His favor was evident in the way he navigated his suffering, ultimately leading to a deeper understanding of God's character and a restored relationship with Him.

Favor As A Source Of Strength

When we face adversity, we may feel weak, discouraged, and ready to give up. However, God's favor is a source of strength that empowers us to keep moving forward. In 2 Corinthians 12:9, Paul writes,

> *"But He said to me, 'My grace is sufficient for you, for My strength is made perfect in weakness."*

This scripture signifies how God's favor is often most evident in our weaknesses, as it is during these times that we rely on His strength rather than our own.

Consider the story of David as he faced adversity. When David was pursued by King Saul, he found himself on the run, living in caves and facing constant danger. Despite these challenges, David continued to seek God, and his favor was evident through the friendships and alliances he formed during this time. God sent him loyal supporters, like Jonathan, who encouraged him and reminded him of God's promises.

David's psalms reflect this dynamic beautifully. In Psalm 34:19, he writes,

> *"Many are the afflictions of the righteous, but the Lord delivers him out of them all."*

David's ability to articulate his struggles and his reliance on God's favor during adversity gave him the strength to endure. He understood that favor does not eliminate challenges, rather, it empowers us to face them head-on with faith.

Overcoming Setbacks and Delays Through Favor

- **The Nature of Setbacks and Delays**

Setbacks and delays are an inevitable part of life. We all face moments when our plans are thwarted, our progress is halted, or we encounter obstacles that seem insurmountable. These experiences can lead to frustration, disappointment, and even doubt. However, it is crucial to recognize that setbacks do not negate God's favor; rather, they can serve as a platform for God to demonstrate His power and purpose in our lives.

In the life of the Israelites, we see how favor operates even in the face of significant setbacks. After being delivered from slavery in Egypt, the Israelites found themselves trapped between the Red Sea and the pursuing Egyptian army. It seemed like a hopeless situation, but God's favor intervened. In Exodus 14:13-14, Moses reassured the people, saying, *"Do not be afraid. Stand still, and see the salvation of the Lord… For the Egyptians whom you see today, you shall see again no more forever. The Lord will fight for you, and you shall hold your peace."*

God's favor manifested in that moment, leading to the miraculous parting of the Red Sea. The Israelites walked through on dry ground, while their enemies were swallowed by the returning waters. This event not only marked a pivotal moment in their journey but also demonstrated that setbacks can become setups for divine intervention when we trust in God's favor.

• **The Importance of Perspective**

Overcoming setbacks requires a shift in perspective. Instead of viewing obstacles as roadblocks, we must recognize them as opportunities for growth and transformation. When faced with setbacks, it is easy to succumb to discouragement and despair. However, maintaining a perspective of faith enables us to see God's favor at work even when circumstances are challenging.

In the New Testament, we see this principle illustrated in the life of Apostle Paul. Paul faced numerous setbacks in his ministry, shipwrecks, imprisonments, and physical hardships. Yet, he continually maintained a perspective of gratitude and faith. In 2 Corinthians 4:17, Paul writes,

"For our light affliction, which is but for a moment, is working for us a far more exceeding and eternal weight of glory."

Paul viewed his setbacks as opportunities for God's glory to be revealed, and his unwavering faith allowed him to overcome adversity.

This perspective of faith allows us to lean into God's favor rather than retreating in fear. When we encounter setbacks, we must remind ourselves that God is still in control, and His favor can turn our difficulties into testimonies of His goodness.

- **Seeking God in Times of Delay**

Delays can be particularly frustrating, as they challenge our patience and understanding of God's timing. However, delays can also be moments where God's favor is at work, preparing us for what lies ahead. In these times, seeking God through prayer and reflection is essential.

The story of Abraham and Sarah illustrates this beautifully. God promised Abraham that he would be the father of many nations, but years passed without the fulfillment of that promise. Despite the delay, God's favor was still present. In Genesis 18:14, God asked, *"Is anything too hard for the Lord?"* This question serves as a reminder that even in times of waiting, God is sovereign and His plans will not fail.

During periods of delay, it is important to trust in God's timing. Instead of rushing ahead with our plans or taking matters into our own hands, we must seek God's guidance and wisdom. Favor is often revealed in the waiting, as God prepares our hearts and minds for the next season of our lives.

Staying Aligned With God's Plan During Tough Times

- **The Importance of Alignment**

Staying aligned with God's plan during tough times is crucial for experiencing favor in adversity. When challenges arise, it can be tempting to lose sight of God's purpose or become discouraged. However, remaining focused on God's promises and seeking His direction is essential for navigating difficult seasons.

In the story of Joseph, we see how alignment with God's plan played a critical role in his ability to endure adversity. Despite being betrayed, sold into slavery, and imprisoned, Joseph remained faithful to God. He consistently sought to honor God in his actions, whether in Potiphar's house or in the prison. His alignment with God's purpose allowed him to interpret dreams, ultimately leading him to a position of high favor in Egypt.

Joseph's experience teaches us that our response to adversity matters. Instead of becoming bitter or resentful, we must choose to trust God's plan, believing that He can work all things together for our good (Romans 8:28). This trust opens the door for favor to flow, even in the midst of trials.

• The Role of Faith in Adversity

Faith is an important component of staying aligned with God's plan during tough times. When faced with challenges, our faith can be tested, leading to doubts and fears. However, maintaining a strong foundation of faith allows us to see beyond our circumstances and trust in God's goodness.

In Hebrews 11:1, we are reminded that

> *"faith is the substance of things hoped for, the evidence of things not seen."*

This verse emphasizes that faith is not reliant on visible outcomes; rather, it is rooted in a deep trust in God's character and promises. When we encounter adversity, it is essential to reaffirm our faith, reminding ourselves of God's faithfulness in the past and His commitment to our future.

During trials, we can strengthen our faith by immersing ourselves in God's word, prayer, and worship. The stories of biblical figures who endured adversity serve as powerful reminders of God's faithfulness and favor. Reflecting on these testimonies can bolster our faith and encourage us to persevere through our own challenges.

• Embracing God's Presence in Tough Times

In times of adversity, seeking God's presence is vital for staying aligned with His plan. God promises to be with us in our struggles, providing comfort and guidance. In Isaiah 41:10, He reassures us,

"Fear not, for I am with you; be not dismayed, for I am your God. I will strengthen you, yes, I will help you; I will uphold you with My righteous right hand."

When we face adversity, embracing God's presence allows us to experience His favor in powerful ways. It reminds us that we are not alone, and His strength is made perfect in our weakness. During challenging times, it is essential to prioritize our relationship with God, seeking His wisdom and comfort through prayer, meditation, and worship.

The story of Apostle Paul provides an excellent example of this. While imprisoned for his faith, Paul remained focused on his mission and continued to spread the Gospel. Instead of allowing his circumstances to deter him, he embraced God's presence and purpose, writing letters of encouragement to the early church. Paul's faithfulness in the midst of adversity resulted in profound impact, as many came to faith through his witness.

Favor is often most evident during our most challenging moments. Trials and setbacks provide opportunities for God's grace and support to manifest in profound ways. By recognizing how favor operates during adversity, we can overcome setbacks and delays with renewed hope and strength.

Staying aligned with God's plan during tough times requires a commitment to faith, prayer, and embracing His presence. As we handle adversity, we must remember that God's favor is not absent; it is present, ready to empower us to fulfill our divine assignments.

Favor in adversity is a testament to God's faithfulness,

demonstrating that even in our struggles, He is working for our good. By trusting in His promises and maintaining our alignment with His will, we can experience favor that sustains us through every trial.

CHAPTER FIVE

HOW TO UNLOCK FAVOR THROUGH VISION

◆ ◆ ◆

The Importance of
Visionary Thinking

V isionary thinking is essential for unlocking favor in our lives. It is the ability to see beyond our current circumstances and envision a future filled with possibilities. A clear vision shapes our actions, inspires our decisions, and fuels our motivation. It is an integral part of living a purpose-driven life, particularly when we seek to walk in God's favor.

At its core, vision is about perceiving the future as God intends it for us. It is having clarity about what we are called to do and the direction in which we should move. Proverbs 29:18 states, *"Where there is no vision, the people perish."* This scripture emphasizes the vital role of vision in our lives. Without a clear vision, we can become aimless, lost in distractions, and unable to fulfill our God-given purpose.

Having a God-given vision is crucial for experiencing favor. God often places dreams and aspirations in our hearts that align with His purposes. When we embrace this vision, we position ourselves to receive favors that empower us to achieve what we cannot do on our own.

For example, Joseph had a vision in the form of dreams that revealed his future prominence. Despite facing betrayal and imprisonment, Joseph remained focused on his vision. His ability to hold onto that vision, despite dire circumstances, allowed him to access God's favor. Ultimately, Joseph's faithfulness and visionary thinking led to his promotion in Egypt, where he saved countless lives during a famine.

The Connection Between Vision And Favor

Vision and favor are intertwined. When you have a clear and compelling vision, you position yourself to attract favor. Favor is drawn to those who dare to dream and aspire for greatness. It is essential to recognize that visionary thinking goes hand in hand with faith.

Thinking big opens the door to possibilities that may seem impossible in the natural. It requires us to step outside of our comfort zones and trust in God's ability to accomplish more than we can ask or think (Ephesians 3:20). When we limit our vision to what seems attainable, we may miss out on the greater blessings that God desires to pour into our lives.

For instance, during his early reign, King Solomon exemplified visionary thinking. When God appeared to Solomon in a dream and asked what he wanted, Solomon did not ask for wealth or a long life; instead, he asked for wisdom to govern God's people effectively (1 Kings 3:5-9). This visionary request pleased God, who granted Solomon not only wisdom but also riches and honor beyond what any king had ever known. Solomon's visionary thinking unlocked extraordinary levels of favor that positioned him as one of the most revered kings in history.

The Role Of Prayer In Developing Vision

Developing a God-centered vision requires intentionality and prayer. Seeking God's guidance through prayer helps us discern His will and receive clarity about our purpose. It is essential to create a habit of prayerful reflection, asking God to reveal His plans for our lives.

James 1:5 encourages us,

> *"If any of you lacks wisdom, let him ask of God, who gives to all liberally and without reproach, and it will be given to him."*

This promise assures us that God desires to guide us and reveal the vision He has for us.

When we approach God in prayer, we develop a receptive heart and mind that allows Him to impart His vision. We must be willing to listen, reflect, and act upon what He reveals. This prayerful posture opens the door for divine favor to manifest in our lives as we align our actions with God's vision.

How Thinking Big Unlocks Greater Levels Of Favor

• The Power of Thinking Big

Thinking big is a crucial mindset that can change our lives and unlock greater levels of favor. It requires us to break free from limitations and embrace the possibilities that God has for us. When we think big, we open ourselves to extraordinary opportunities and experiences that align with God's purposes. The power of thinking big comes from the willingness to see beyond the present challenges and to imagine a future shaped by faith, obedience, and a clear vision of God's will.

This mindset encourages us to move beyond mediocrity and step into the fullness of what God has already prepared. It invites us to expand our capacity to dream, to have faith in the impossible, and to pursue greatness as part of God's plan for our lives. Scripture is filled with examples of individuals who embraced a *"think big"* mentality, allowing God to work mightily in their lives.

Breaking Free from Limitations: Thinking big requires breaking free from self-imposed limitations and societal expectations. It means refusing to be confined by past failures, current circumstances, or fear of the unknown. Many of us are held back by limiting beliefs, whether about ourselves, our resources, or what God can do through us. These limitations hinder us from accessing the fullness of God's favor and blessing.

The Bible repeatedly emphasizes the importance of faith that is not limited by human constraints. In Matthew 19:26, Jesus says,

> *"With men, this is impossible, but with God, all things are possible."*

This statement shows that thinking big requires us to align our vision with God's limitless power. When we elevate our thinking, we acknowledge that God is able to do far more than we can ask or imagine (Ephesians 3:20).

A powerful example of this mindset is found in the life of Jabez. In 1 Chronicles 4:10, Jabez prayed,

> *"Oh, that You would bless me indeed, and enlarge my*

territory, that Your hand would be with me, and that You would keep me from evil, that I may not cause pain!"

This bold prayer demonstrates a *"think big"* mentality. Jabez dared to ask God for an expanded vision and greater blessings, and God granted his request. Jabez's story reminds us that when we think big, we position ourselves to receive more of God's favor and to experience His blessings in greater ways.

- **Daring to Dream and Aspire for Greatness**
  Thinking big involves daring to dream and aspiring for greatness. It challenges us to step outside our comfort zones and embrace the fullness of what God has in store. This concept is not about personal ambition or worldly success, rather, it's about aligning our dreams with God's plans and purposes for our lives.

God encourages His people to have big dreams and bold aspirations. Proverbs 29:18 tells us,

"Where there is no vision, the people perish."

Without a clear vision, one that goes beyond the ordinary and aims for the extraordinary, our potential is limited, and we miss out on God's favor. Dreaming big involves trusting that God's plans for us are higher than our own (Isaiah 55:8-9). His plans often require us to stretch beyond what we think is possible, to step out in faith and to pursue a destiny that reflects His greatness in us.

This was true for Abraham. God promised Abraham that He would make him the father of many nations, despite Abraham's advanced age and the barrenness of his wife, Sarah. God called Abraham to dream big and trust in His promise. In Genesis 15:5,

God told Abraham to look up at the stars and count them, saying,

"So shall your descendants be."

Abraham's willingness to believe in God's seemingly impossible promise led to an outpouring of divine favor that blessed not only him but generations to come.

• Faith That Elevates Our Expectations

One of the key elements of thinking big is faith. Faith elevates our expectations and shapes our reality. When we place our faith in God's ability to work through us, we begin to see beyond our current limitations. Faith allows us to envision a future that is greater than our present circumstances. It allows us to expect more from God because we understand that He is able to provide exceedingly and abundantly above all we could ask or think (Ephesians 3:20). The faith that accompanies thinking big is not passive, it requires action. James 2:17 reminds us that

"faith without works is dead."

This means that while we think big, we must also take bold steps of faith toward the vision God has given us. When we act on our faith, we open the door for God's favor to flow into our lives. This principle is illustrated powerfully in the story of Peter walking on water. In Matthew 14:28-29, Peter said to Jesus,

"Lord, if it is You, command me to come to You on the water."

Jesus said, *"Come,"* and Peter stepped out of the boat and walked on water. Peter's faith in Jesus' command allowed him to experience the supernatural. Though Peter eventually faltered, his initial act of thinking big and stepping out in faith allowed him to experience a level of divine favor that others did not.

• Thinking Big Requires Bold Action

Thinking big goes beyond wishful thinking; it requires bold action. The Bible is filled with individuals who thought big and acted boldly, trusting that God would honor their faith. Bold actions are often risky, but they are necessary to unlock new levels of favor. They require us to move beyond what is comfortable or familiar and step into the unknown, trusting that God will guide and sustain us. For example, Nehemiah had a vision to rebuild the walls of Jerusalem. This was an enormous undertaking, and many doubted that it could be done. Yet Nehemiah acted boldly. He sought favor from the king, organized the people, and overcame opposition to accomplish the task (Nehemiah 2:17-20). His ability to think big and take bold action led to the fulfillment of God's plan, and the walls of Jerusalem were rebuilt in just 52 days. David's story provides another powerful example of thinking big and taking bold action. As a young shepherd, David had a vision of becoming a great king and leader. This vision was put to the test when he faced Goliath, a giant who intimidated the entire Israelite army. While others trembled in fear, David saw an opportunity to glorify God. His ability to think beyond the immediate challenge and envision a greater purpose unlocked the favor of God in his life. He declared,

"The Lord who delivered me from the paw of the lion and from the paw of the bear, He will deliver me from the hand

of this Philistine" 1 Samuel 17:37.

David's confidence in God's power enabled him to take bold action. Armed with nothing but a sling and five stones, he defeated Goliath, demonstrating that thinking big, combined with bold faith, leads to extraordinary victories. His triumph marked the beginning of a series of blessings that would ultimately lead him to the throne of Israel.

- **Envisioning God's Greater Purpose**
  Another key aspect of thinking big is the ability to envision God's greater purpose for our lives. Thinking big is not merely about achieving personal success or prosperity. It is about aligning our lives with God's kingdom purposes and understanding how He wants to use us to make an impact in the world. When we think big, we tap into God's overarching plan, which is always greater than what we can see in the moment. Moses, for instance, could have settled for a comfortable life after fleeing from Egypt, but God had a bigger purpose for him. Despite his initial reluctance, Moses embraced God's vision to lead the Israelites out of slavery and into the Promised Land. In Exodus 3:11, Moses questioned his ability to take on such a monumental task, saying,

  "Who am I that I should go to Pharaoh and bring the Israelites out of Egypt?",

  with God's assurance and favor, Moses stepped into the divine plan. His obedience to God's greater purpose unlocked unprecedented favor and led to one of the greatest deliverances in biblical history.

Expanding Your Vision

To unlock greater levels of favor, it is essential to expand your vision. This requires setting ambitious goals and daring to dream beyond your current circumstances. When we limit our vision to what seems achievable, we may miss out on the incredible plans God has for us.

Expanding your vision involves stepping into a mindset of abundance rather than scarcity. God desires to bless us far beyond our expectations. In John 10:10, Jesus says,

"I have come that they may have life, and that they may have it more abundantly."

This abundance is not limited to material wealth; it encompasses every aspect of our lives, spiritual growth, relationships, and opportunities to serve others.

When we broaden our vision and expect great things from God, we align ourselves with His character. God is a God of abundance, and He delights in blessing His children. This mindset attracts favor because it demonstrates our faith in His ability to do exceedingly abundantly above all that we ask or think.

The Role Of Faith In Thinking Big

Thinking big is inherently linked to faith. It requires a belief that God can and will fulfill the visions He places in our hearts. Our faith allows us to see beyond our current circumstances and trust in God's ability to brings our dreams to fruition.

In (Matthew 17:20), Jesus tells us that faith as small as a mustard seed can move mountains. This illustrates that even a little faith can lead to significant results. When we combine our faith with visionary thinking, we position ourselves for God's favor to manifest in powerful ways.

The story of Deborah, the prophetess and judge of Israel, exemplifies this dynamic. In a time of oppression, God called

Deborah to lead her people to victory against their enemies. Her vision was not merely about military success; it was about restoring God's justice among the people.

Deborah's faith and vision inspired Barak, the military leader, to follow her command. Despite the apparent odds against them, Deborah's confidence in God's plan led to a miraculous victory. This example demonstrates that when we embrace our vision with faith, we can unlock favor that leads to extraordinary outcomes.

Examples Of Visionary Leaders Who Accessed High Favor

• David: The Visionary King

David stands as one of the most prominent examples of a visionary leader who accessed high levels of favor through his unwavering faith and bold thinking. From his humble beginnings as a shepherd boy in the fields of Bethlehem to his reign as the greatest king of Israel, David's life was marked by a visionary mindset that transcended the limitations of his circumstances. His ability to see beyond the immediate challenges, coupled with his deep faith in God, unlocked extraordinary favor and shaped the course of history.

David's journey toward kingship began long before he was anointed by the prophet Samuel. As a young boy tending to his father's sheep, David spent countless hours alone in the fields. It was during these solitary moments that his relationship with God deepened, and his vision for greatness began to take shape. Far from being idle, these moments became opportunities for David to develop trust in God, develop his skills, and prepare for a future that, at the time, seemed unimaginable.

As a shepherd, David was responsible for protecting the sheep from wild animals. His encounters with lions and bears not only developed his physical abilities but also nurtured his faith in God's protection and provision. David learned to rely on God in life-threatening situations, and this trust in God's deliverance was a critical factor in shaping his vision for the future. His experience as a shepherd was not just a training ground for leadership but a time when his faith grew stronger and his vision for what God could do through him expanded.

David's vision was not limited by his circumstances. Even though he was the youngest of his brothers and seemingly insignificant in the eyes of his family, he never allowed his position to define his potential. This is a crucial lesson for anyone aspiring to experience greater levels of favor: vision is not dictated by where you start, but by your ability to see what God has in store for you.

- **The Goliath Moment**: Vision in Action, David's visionary mindset became fully evident in his encounter with Goliath, the Philistine giant who terrorized the Israelite army. While the entire Israelite army was paralyzed by fear, including King Saul, David stepped forward with boldness and confidence. His vision allowed him to see the situation differently than everyone else. Where others saw an insurmountable obstacle, David saw an opportunity to glorify God and demonstrate His power. David's confidence did not come from his own strength or abilities but from his faith in God. In 1 Samuel 17:37, David declared,

- *"The Lord who delivered me from the paw of the lion and from the paw of the bear, He will deliver me from the hand of this Philistine."*

- David's past experiences of God's faithfulness in smaller battles gave him the faith to believe in victory against a much larger adversary. His visionary thinking, his ability to see beyond the immediate threat and trust in God's larger plan, set him apart from the rest of the Israelite army. David's decision to face Goliath was not just an act of courage, it was a demonstration of visionary leadership. He did not wait for someone else to take action, he recognized that God had positioned him for such a moment. This is a hallmark of visionary leaders, they see opportunities where others see only challenges, and they are willing to take bold action because of their faith in God's ability to bring about victory. The result of David's bold thinking and faith was a decisive victory that not only secured the safety of Israel but also established David as a leader among his people. His triumph over Goliath became the catalyst for a series of blessings and opportunities that would ultimately lead him to the throne. This moment in David's life illustrates that visionary thinking, when combined with faith in God, unlocks divine favor and positions us for extraordinary outcomes.

- **The Favor of Leadership and Influence:** David's journey to becoming king was not immediate, but his visionary mindset continued to guide him through the challenges that followed his victory over Goliath. After his triumph, David gained favor with King Saul and became a warrior in Saul's army. However, as David's popularity grew, so did Saul's jealousy, leading to a prolonged period of conflict between the two men. Despite these challenges, David's vision of becoming king remained intact, and he continued to walk in obedience to God. Even while being pursued by Saul, David demonstrated remarkable restraint and integrity. On multiple occasions, David had the opportunity to kill Saul and seize the throne by force, but he refused to do so, recognizing that it was not yet God's appointed time for him to reign. David's vision was not just about achieving power; it was about fulfilling God's purpose in God's timing. This patience and reliance on God's plan further unlocked divine favor in David's life. David's eventual ascension to the throne was marked by favor that extended beyond personal success. His visionary leadership enabled him to unite the twelve tribes of Israel, something that had never been accomplished before. Under his reign, Israel became a strong and unified nation, experiencing peace, prosperity, and military success. David's ability to think beyond immediate challenges and work toward a greater vision for his people was a key factor in the favor he received as king.

One of David's most significant achievements as king was his establishment of Jerusalem as the capital of Israel and the center of worship for the nation. David envisioned a place where the people of Israel could gather to worship God and where the Ark of the Covenant could be housed. This vision led to the eventual construction of the temple by his son Solomon, but it was David's heart for worship and his desire to honor God that laid the foundation for this monumental achievement.

- **David's Heart for Worship:** A Key to Favor: Another critical aspect of David's visionary leadership was his heart for worship. Throughout his life, David maintained a deep relationship with God, expressed most profoundly through his psalms of worship and praise. David's love for God and his commitment to honoring Him through worship unlocked a unique level of favor. His psalms reflect a man who not only sought God's favor but also desired to glorify God in all that he did. David's heart for worship was evident when he brought the Ark of the Covenant to Jerusalem. In (2 Samuel 6), we read that David danced before the Lord with all his might, unashamed of what others might think. His exuberant worship demonstrated his deep reverence for God and his understanding that God's favor is connected to a heart of worship. David's willingness to worship God with total abandon positioned him to receive even greater levels of favor throughout his reign. David's psalms have continued to inspire us believers for generations. His honesty, vulnerability, and trust in God, even in times of great distress, serve as a model for how we, too, can experience God's favor through worship. Whether in times of victory or trial, David's life shows us that a heart of worship unlocks the favor of God in profound ways.

- **Leaving a Legacy of Vision and Favor:** David's visionary leadership and the favor he experienced did not end with his reign, it left a lasting legacy that continues to impact the world today. David's line was chosen by God to bring forth the Messiah, Jesus Christ. In 2 Samuel 7:16, God promised David,

"Your house and your kingdom shall endure forever before me; your throne shall be established forever."

This covenant established David's legacy as one of eternal significance. David's life teaches us that visionary thinking, when aligned with God's purposes, leaves a legacy that transcends time. His vision for Israel, his heart for worship, and his faith in God's promises shaped the future of his nation and laid the foundation for the coming of Christ. David's example reminds us that the favor we receive when we think big and act boldly is not just for our benefit; it is meant to impact future generations and advance God's kingdom.

Deborah: A Courageous Leader

Deborah, the prophetess and judge of Israel, stands as a remarkable example of a visionary leader who accessed high favor through her faith, wisdom, and courage. In a time when Israel was under the oppressive rule of the Canaanite king Jabin and his commander Sisera, God raised Deborah to lead the nation into victory. Her leadership was not only instrumental in military success but also in restoring justice and righteousness to a nation that had turned away from God. Deborah's story, found in Judges 4-5, demonstrates the power of visionary thinking and courageous faith in unlocking divine favor for herself and her people.

During Deborah's time, Israel was suffering under severe oppression. For twenty years, Jabin's army, led by Sisera, had terrorized the Israelites, rendering them powerless and fearful. The people of Israel cried out to God for deliverance, and Deborah was chosen as the vessel through whom this deliverance would come. As both a prophetess and a judge, Deborah held a unique position of authority, guiding Israel spiritually and politically. Her ability to lead in both capacities highlights her extraordinary vision and faith.

What sets Deborah apart as a visionary leader was her willingness to rise above the societal expectations of her time. In an era when leadership was predominantly male, Deborah's position as a female judge and prophetess speaks to her courage and obedience to God's calling. She did not let societal norms limit her vision or her ability to lead. Instead, she embraced her role with confidence, knowing that God had placed her in this position for such a time as this.

Deborah's leadership was characterized by her ability to inspire faith and action in others. One of the most significant moments in her story is when she called Barak, a military commander, to lead Israel's army against Sisera. Barak was hesitant, fearing the strength of Sisera's forces, which included 900 iron chariots. However, Deborah cast a clear vision of victory, reminding Barak of God's promise to deliver Sisera into their hands.

In Judges 4:6-7, Deborah conveyed God's plan, saying,

> *"Has not the Lord, the God of Israel, commanded you? Go, take with you ten thousand men of Naphtali and Zebulun and lead them up to Mount Tabor. I will lead Sisera, the commander of Jabin's army, with his chariots and his troops to the Kishon River and give him into your hands."*

Despite Barak's fear, Deborah's unwavering faith in God's ability to deliver Israel emboldened him to take action. Her vision of victory extended beyond military success; it was rooted in her understanding of God's sovereignty and His desire to restore Israel.

Barak, encouraged by Deborah's faith, agreed to lead the army, but he insisted that Deborah accompany him into battle. This request highlights the trust and respect Deborah had earned as a leader. Barak recognized that Deborah's presence, and more importantly, her connection to God, would be key to their success. Deborah agreed, knowing that the victory would ultimately belong to God, not to human strength.

Deborah's visionary leadership and courageous faith unlocked divine favor not just for herself but for the entire nation of Israel. Under her leadership, Barak and the Israelite army defeated Sisera's forces, despite the overwhelming odds. Sisera fled on foot, only to be killed by Jael, a woman who played a pivotal role in completing Israel's victory. This unexpected turn of events highlighted that the victory was orchestrated by God and was a testament to the faith of the women who trusted Him.

The outcome of the battle, as described in Judges 5, was not just military success but a time of peace and restoration for Israel. Deborah's leadership brought an end to twenty years of oppression, and as a result of her visionary thinking, the land had rest for forty years (Judges 5:31). Her ability to mobilize the nation, inspire courage, and trust in God's promises demonstrates the transformative power of visionary leadership.

Deborah's story continues to inspire believers today. She was a leader who did not let fear or societal limitations hinder her from stepping into her God-given role. Her vision extended beyond the immediate challenge of defeating Sisera; she saw a future where Israel would be free from oppression and restored to righteousness. Her faith in God's ability to deliver the nation unlocked a level of favor that not only secured military victory but also brought lasting peace.

Deborah's life teaches us that visionary thinking, when paired with faith and courage, can mobilize a community toward a common purpose and unlock doors of favor that bless an entire generation. Like Deborah, we are called to trust in God's promises, step into leadership when needed, and embrace the vision He has for our lives.

The legacies of David and Deborah therefore serve as powerful reminders of the impact that visionary leaders can have on their communities and nations. When we embrace visionary thinking, we create opportunities for God's favor to flow not only into our lives but also into the lives of those around us.

Visionary leaders challenge the status quo and inspire others to think bigger. They create an environment where God's favor can flourish, allowing their communities to experience transformation and growth.

As we reflect on these examples, we are reminded that each of us has the potential to be a visionary leader in our own right. By seeking God's guidance, aligning our vision with His purposes, and stepping out in faith, we can unlock favor that extends beyond our individual lives to impact future generations.

Unlocking favor through vision is a process that requires us to think beyond our current circumstances and embrace the possibilities God has for us. Visionary thinking opens the door for greater levels of favor, as it aligns us with God's purposes and prepares us to fulfill our divine assignments.

As we have seen in this chapter, the examples of visionary leaders like David and Deborah remind us that with faith and boldness, we can access high favor and make a lasting impact. The journey toward unlocking favor begins with a clear vision and the willingness to pursue it, no matter the cost.

CHAPTER SIX

CULTIVATING
A HEART THAT
ATTRACTS FAVOR

◆ ◆ ◆

The Role of Obedience and
Humility in Securing Favor

F avor is not only a gift from God but also something that we can position ourselves to receive through our heart posture. Two key traits that consistently attract divine favor are obedience and humility. These qualities reflect a heart that is aligned with God's will and ready to receive and steward His blessings effectively.

Obedience As The Foundation Of Favor

Obedience is a critical factor in attracting and securing divine favor. Throughout Scripture, we see that when individuals obey God's commands and directives, they position themselves to receive His favor. Obedience is more than just following rules, it is about surrendering to God's will and trusting that His way is the best path for us.

One of the clearest examples of how obedience secures favor is seen in the life of Abraham. God commanded Abraham to leave his homeland and go to a place He would show him. Without knowing exactly where he was going or what lay ahead, Abraham obeyed God's call. This act of obedience became the foundation for the covenant blessings Abraham would receive. Genesis 12:2-3 records God's promise to Abraham

"I will make you a great nation; I will bless you and make your name great; and you shall be a blessing... And in you all the families of the earth shall be blessed."

Abraham's willingness to obey without hesitation led to generational favor. His obedience did not just secure blessings for himself, but it opened the door for his descendants to walk in divine favor. This principle is still true for us today: when we choose to obey God, even in the face of uncertainty, we position ourselves for the outpouring of His favor.

Humility as the Key to Sustaining Favor
While obedience is foundational for securing favor, humility is crucial for sustaining it. Humility reflects a heart that is dependent on God, acknowledging that all blessings come from Him and not from our own efforts. God's word is clear about the importance of humility,

"God resists the proud, but gives grace to the humble" (James 4:6).

Humility keeps us in a position where we can continue to receive and steward God's favor. It guards against the pride that can arise when we experience success or blessings. King David is a prime example of how humility attracts favor. Even after being anointed as king and experiencing many victories, David maintained a humble heart before God. In Psalm 51:17, he wrote,

"The sacrifices of God are a broken spirit, a broken and contrite

heart, these, O God, You will not despise."

David's humility allowed him to remain in God's favor throughout his life, despite his shortcomings. When he sinned, he quickly repented and sought God's mercy, acknowledging his dependence on God's grace. This humility not only preserved David's favor but also ensured that his legacy of favor would continue through his descendants.

The Consequences of Disobedience and Pride

Just as obedience and humility attract favor, disobedience, and pride repel it. The Bible is full of examples where individuals lost God's favor because of their disobedience or pride. While God desires to bless His people, He also expects them to walk in submission to His will. When we choose to go our own way, we not only forfeit the blessings He has prepared for us but also open ourselves up to the consequences of rebellion. The story of King Saul, the first king of Israel, serves as a powerful warning in this regard. Saul was chosen by God, and he initially walked in favor. However, his disobedience and pride led to his downfall, demonstrating that no position or status can shield us from the consequences of disregarding God's commands.

Saul's story begins with great promise. Chosen by God to lead Israel, Saul started his reign with the favor of both God and man. He was given the responsibility to unite the nation and lead them in battle against their enemies. However, Saul's trajectory took a dramatic turn when he failed to obey God's instructions regarding the destruction of the Amalekites. In (1 Samuel 15:3), God commanded Saul to completely destroy the Amalekites and their possessions, leaving nothing behind. Instead, Saul spared the Amalekite king and the best of the livestock, deciding to offer them as sacrifices to God. In doing so, Saul disobeyed God's direct command.

This moment is critical because it reveals Saul's misunderstanding of obedience. Saul thought that offering a sacrifice would compensate for his disobedience. He failed to recognize that God values obedience above all else. In 1 Samuel 15:22, the prophet Samuel confronted Saul, saying,

> *"Has the Lord as great delight in burnt offerings and sacrifices, as in obeying the voice of the Lord? Behold, to obey is better than sacrifice, and to heed than the fat of rams."*

Samuel's words highlight the core issue, Saul placed his own judgment above God's instructions, thinking he could modify God's command and still earn His favor.

The Seriousness Of Disobedience

Saul's failure to obey God's clear instructions had devastating consequences. God rejected him as king, stripping him of the favor and blessing he had once enjoyed. This decision was not made lightly; it was the result of Saul's persistent disobedience and disregard for God's authority. In 1 Samuel 15:23, Samuel delivers God's judgment on Saul,

> *"For rebellion is as the sin of witchcraft, and stubbornness is as iniquity and idolatry. Because you have rejected the word of the Lord, He also has rejected you from being king."*

This passage shows the seriousness of disobedience. Saul's failure to follow God's command cost him not only his kingship but also God's favor. His rebellion is compared to witchcraft, and his stubbornness to idolatry, strong terms that emphasize how God views disobedience. Saul's actions were not just mistakes; they were acts of defiance against God's will. Disobedience is not merely failing to meet a standard, it is an active rejection of God's authority and His rightful place as Lord of our lives.

The Role Of Pride In Saul's Downfall

Saul's disobedience was compounded by his pride. Instead of acknowledging his mistake and repenting, Saul justified his actions and attempted to shift the blame onto others. In 1 Samuel 15:15, when Samuel confronted Saul about why he had spared the livestock, Saul responded,

> *"The people spared the best of the sheep and oxen, to sacrifice to the Lord your God."*

Saul's response reveals his unwillingness to take responsibility for his actions, choosing instead to blame the people under his command. This pride, coupled with his disobedience, further distanced Saul from God.

Pride is dangerous because it blinds us to our own faults and leads us to believe that we are above correction. Saul's pride in thinking he could offer sacrifices on his own terms, rather than waiting for the prophet Samuel, showed that he valued his own ways above God's. This self-reliance and arrogance ultimately led to his rejection by God. Saul's story reminds us that pride is a direct barrier to receiving God's favor. As Proverbs 16:18 warns,

> *"Pride goes before destruction and a haughty spirit before a fall."*

The Ripple Effect Of Disobedience And Pride

Saul's disobedience did not only affect him, it had far-reaching consequences for the nation of Israel. As their king, Saul's actions set the tone for the entire nation. His failure to follow

God's command opened the door to instability and conflict, and ultimately, Saul's reign ended in disgrace. His disobedience left a legacy of strife, as seen in the later divisions and battles that plagued Israel.

Moreover, Saul's pride prevented him from repenting and seeking restoration. Unlike David, who later became king and repented deeply after his own sins, Saul clung to his pride and continued down a path of self-destruction. His refusal to humble himself before God led to increasing paranoia, jealousy, and irrational behavior, as seen in his pursuit of David. Saul's story is a reminder that pride, when left unchecked, can destroy not only our relationship with God but also our relationships with others and the legacy we leave behind.

Saul's downfall teaches us the importance of humility and repentance. While Saul refused to repent, other biblical figures, such as David, show us the power of humbling ourselves before God. When David sinned, he quickly acknowledged his wrongs and sought God's forgiveness. This willingness to repent and seek God's mercy is a key difference between David and Saul. David's humility restored his relationship with God, while Saul's pride led to his downfall.

As believers, we are called to walk in humility and obedience, recognizing that God's ways are higher than our own. Disobedience and pride cut us off from the flow of God's favor, while humility and a repentant heart open the door for restoration and blessing. James 4:6 reminds us,

"God resists the proud, but gives grace to the humble."

When we choose humility over pride and obedience over self-will, we position ourselves to receive the full measure of God's favor.

The story of King Saul serves as a sobering reminder of the consequences of disobedience and pride. Though Saul began his reign with God's favor, his failure to obey and his refusal to humble himself before God led to his rejection as king. Saul's disobedience cost him not only his position but also the opportunity to leave a lasting legacy of righteousness.

We must learn from Saul's example and take seriously the call to walk in obedience and humility. God's favor is available to those who submit to His will and acknowledge their dependence on Him. Disobedience and pride, however, will always lead to separation from God's favor and blessing. Let us strive to live in obedience to God's word, recognizing that true greatness comes not from pride or self-reliance, but from humble submission to our Creator.

Humility and obedience are essential because they reflect a heart that is submitted to God's will. When we walk in these qualities, we create an environment where favor can flourish. By surrendering our will to God and maintaining a humble spirit, we open the door for continued blessings and favor.

Prayers And Declarations For Attracting Divine Favor

Prayer is a powerful tool for attracting divine favor. Through prayer, we communicate with God, express our desires, and align our hearts with His will. Declarations are also important because they are a form of faith-filled confession that allows us to speak God's promises over our lives. In this section, we will explore prayers and declarations that can help position us to receive and walk in favor.

Prayer For Divine Alignment

Heavenly Father, I thank You for the gift of Your favor. I

acknowledge that every good and perfect gift comes from You. Today, I ask for Your guidance in aligning my heart and actions with Your will. Help me to walk in obedience to Your commands, and give me the wisdom to discern Your voice in every situation.

Lord, I ask for a heart of humility. Keep me from pride and self-sufficiency, and remind me daily that without You, I can do nothing. Teach me to trust You in all things and to rely on Your strength rather than my own. I invite Your favor into every area of my life, my relationships, my work, my ministry, and my personal growth.

Father, as I seek to walk in obedience and humility, I pray that Your favor will go before me and open doors that no man can shut. Let Your presence surround me like a shield, and may everything I do be a reflection of Your glory. In Jesus' name, Amen.

Declaration Of Favor In Every Area

- I declare that I am highly favored by God, and His blessings are overtaking me.
- I declare that the favor of God is surrounding me like a shield, and I am walking in His divine protection and guidance.
- I declare that doors of opportunity are opening for me, and I am stepping into new levels of favor and influence.
- I declare that favor is following me in every area of my life, my career, my relationships, my finances, and my spiritual walk.
- I declare that as I walk in obedience to God's word, I am experiencing His favor in ways I never imagined.
- I declare that God's favor is positioning me for promotion, breakthrough, and divine connections.
- I declare that humility is my posture, and I am

dependent on God for every blessing and success I experience.

These prayers and declarations powerfully align our hearts with God's promises. When we speak these words in faith, we invite God's favor into our lives and create an atmosphere where blessings can flow freely.

The Power Of Daily Declarations

Making daily declarations of favor is a practice that can transform our mindset and spiritual posture. Declarations are more than just positive affirmations; they are grounded in God's word and reflect His promises for our lives. When we speak these declarations, we align ourselves with God's will and set the stage for His favor to manifest.

In Proverbs 18:21, we are reminded that

"death and life are in the power of the tongue."

This means that what we speak has the ability to shape our reality. By declaring God's favor over our lives, we are speaking life into our circumstances and positioning ourselves to receive His blessings.

One way to incorporate declarations into your daily routine is to set aside a few minutes each morning to speak them over your life. As you do this consistently, you will begin to see a shift in your mindset and circumstances. Favor is not just about receiving material blessings, it is about walking in the fullness of God's purpose and experiencing His goodness in every area of your life.

Prayer For A Humble Heart

Heavenly Father, I come before You with a heart of gratitude. I acknowledge that all I have comes from You, and I ask that You keep me humble in all circumstances. Lord, remove any pride or self-reliance from my heart, and help me to depend fully on You.

Teach me to walk in humility and to serve others as Christ served. Let my actions reflect a heart that is submitted to Your will, and let Your favor rest upon me as I seek to honor You in all I do. I declare that humility will be my guide, and through it, I will experience the fullness of Your blessings. In Jesus' name, Amen.

Stories Of Those Who Attracted Favor Through Their Heart Posture

Throughout the Bible, we find examples of individuals who attracted favor because of the posture of their hearts. Their stories demonstrate that when we walk in obedience, humility, and faith, we position ourselves for divine favor that transcends circumstances and transforms lives. In this section, we will look at two key figures: Cyrus and Ruth.

Cyrus: A Heart For God's Purpose

Cyrus, the king of Persia, stands as one of the most remarkable examples of a non-Israelite ruler who attracted God's favor. His story is a testimony to how God's purposes transcend human boundaries, using even those outside the covenant community to accomplish His divine will. Despite being a pagan king, Cyrus was chosen by God to play a pivotal role in the restoration of Israel after the Babylonian exile. His reign is a perfect demonstration of how favor is not limited by human expectation, nationality, or religious background but is granted to those whom God selects for His purposes.

Long before Cyrus was born, the prophet Isaiah prophesied that God would raise up a deliverer to free His people from captivity.

In Isaiah 44:28, God says,

> *"Who says of Cyrus, 'He is My shepherd, and he shall perform all My pleasure, saying to Jerusalem, 'You shall be built,' and to the temple, 'Your foundation shall be laid.'"*

This prophecy, made around 150 years before Cyrus came to power, specifically names him as the one who would restore Jerusalem and rebuild the temple. Isaiah 45:1 further emphasizes Cyrus' role,

> *"Thus says the Lord to His anointed, to Cyrus, whose right hand I have held, to subdue nations before him and loose the armor of kings, to open before him the double doors, so that the gates will not be shut."*

The naming of Cyrus long before his birth reveals the sovereignty of God over history. God knew that this future king, although not part of Israel, would be instrumental in fulfilling His plan for His people. The prophecy also highlights the depth of God's favor, Cyrus was *"anointed"* by God, a term usually reserved for kings of Israel or prophets, indicating the significant role he would play.

Cyrus' Rise To Power And The Conquest Of Babylon

Cyrus' favor was evident in his meteoric rise to power. He was a skilled military strategist and leader who expanded the Persian Empire to become one of the largest in history at that time. In 539 BC, Cyrus captured Babylon, which had been the dominant power in the region and the nation responsible for exiling the

Jews from their homeland. The conquest of Babylon was pivotal not only in establishing Cyrus' rule over the region but also in fulfilling the prophecy regarding the deliverance of the Jewish people.

One key element of Cyrus' success was the favor of God, who orchestrated events to allow his rise to power. God had planned for Cyrus to become king so that he could facilitate the return of the Jewish exiles to Jerusalem. In Isaiah 45:2-3, God speaks directly to Cyrus through the prophecy,

> *"I will go before you and make the crooked places straight; I will break in pieces the gates of bronze and cut the bars of iron. I will give you the treasures of darkness and hidden riches of secret places, that you may know that I, the Lord, who calls you by your name, am the God of Israel."*

These verses illustrate how God actively worked on Cyrus' behalf, ensuring that his military campaigns were successful. God's favor was evident in how easily Babylon fell to the Persians. The gates of the city were left open, allowing Cyrus' army to enter without resistance, fulfilling Isaiah's prophecy of *"the double doors"* being opened.

The Decree Of Cyrus: A Heart Moved By God

Perhaps the most significant aspect of Cyrus' story is his decree allowing the Jewish exiles to return to Jerusalem and rebuild the temple. This event is recorded in the opening verses of the book of Ezra. In Ezra 1:1-2, it states,

> *"Now in the first year of Cyrus king of Persia, that the word of the Lord by the mouth of Jeremiah might be fulfilled, the Lord stirred up the spirit of Cyrus king of*

Persia, so that he made a proclamation throughout all his kingdom, and also put it in writing, saying, 'Thus says Cyrus king of Persia: All the kingdoms of the earth the Lord God of heaven has given me. And He has commanded me to build Him a house at Jerusalem which is in Judah."

The phrase *"the Lord stirred up the spirit of Cyrus"* indicates that God was directly involved in moving Cyrus' heart toward this monumental decision. Despite being a pagan king, Cyrus acknowledged the Lord God of heaven, recognizing that his success and power were a result of divine intervention. This acknowledgement of God's sovereignty was a key reason why Cyrus attracted divine favor. By aligning his actions with God's will, Cyrus played a pivotal role in the fulfillment of biblical prophecy.

Cyrus not only issued the decree but also supported the rebuilding of the temple by returning the sacred temple vessels that Nebuchadnezzar had taken from Jerusalem. He provided resources and protection for the Jewish people as they returned to their homeland. This act of generosity and support further demonstrated that Cyrus had indeed found favor with God, as he became an instrument in fulfilling God's plan.

The Impact Of Cyrus' Leadership

Cyrus' leadership had a lasting impact on the Jewish people and the history of Israel. His decree marked the end of the Babylonian exile, a period of great suffering and displacement for the Jewish people. Through Cyrus' actions, the exiles were not only allowed to return to their homeland but were also able to restore their religious practices and rebuild the temple, the center of Jewish worship.

The rebuilding of the temple in Jerusalem was a significant

moment in Israel's history, symbolizing the restoration of God's covenant people. Cyrus' role in this process demonstrates that God can use anyone, regardless of their background or belief system, to fulfill His purposes. Cyrus' favor with God was not based on his religious identity but on his willingness to act in alignment with God's plans. His story is a powerful reminder that God's favor transcends human expectations and can be extended to those He chooses, even when they are outside the conventional boundaries of faith.

Cyrus' Legacy of Favor: Cyrus' legacy is one of favor, not just for himself but for an entire nation. His leadership and decree set the stage for the restoration of Israel, and his actions continue to be remembered in both Jewish and Christian traditions. Isaiah's prophecy about Cyrus being God's *"shepherd"* emphasizes the idea that God can use anyone, whether they are aware of it or not, to shepherd His people and accomplish His will. More so, Cyrus' story teaches us that favor is not always about personal blessing but about being used by God to bless others. Cyrus was a king of immense power and wealth, yet his greatest contribution was in how he allowed himself to be used by God for the benefit of a people not his own. This act of selflessness and obedience to divine prompting is what sets Cyrus apart as a leader who attracted God's favor.

Ruth: A Heart Of Loyalty And Humility

Ruth is another example of someone who attracted favor because of her heart posture. As a Moabite widow, Ruth faced numerous challenges, including poverty and the loss of her husband. However, her loyalty to her mother-in-law, Naomi, and her humility in seeking refuge under God's protection set her apart.

In Ruth 2:12, Boaz, a wealthy landowner, speaks of Ruth's faithfulness, saying,

"The Lord repay your work, and a full reward be given you by the Lord God of Israel, under whose wings you have come for refuge."

Ruth's decision to stay with Naomi and follow the God of Israel demonstrated her heart of loyalty and humility, which ultimately attracted Boaz's favor.

Ruth's story culminates in her becoming the great-grandmother of King David, positioning her in the lineage of Jesus Christ. Her humility and loyalty not only secured favor in her immediate circumstances but also left a lasting legacy. Ruth's story reminds us that favor often flows through a heart that is willing to serve others and submit to God's will, even in difficult circumstances.

Lessons From Cyrus And Ruth

Both Cyrus and Ruth exemplify the power of heart posture in attracting divine favor. Cyrus's openness to being used by God and Ruth's humility and loyalty show us that God's favor is not reserved for those with perfect lives or backgrounds. Instead, favor flows to those whose hearts are aligned with God's purposes.

The key takeaway from their stories is that favor is not just about external success or blessings, it is about being in the right position to partner with God in accomplishing His plans. When we develop a heart that is obedient, humble, and loyal, we open ourselves to experiencing God's favor in ways that go beyond our expectations.

Having a heart that attracts favor requires obedience, humility, and a willingness to align our actions with God's purposes. Through the examples of individuals like Abraham, David, Cyrus, and Ruth, we see that favor is not an accident, it is a result of a heart that is surrendered to God's will.

As we develop obedience and humility in our lives, we position ourselves for divine favor that not only blesses us but also impacts those around us. By aligning our hearts with God's purposes, we open the door for His favor to flow freely, transforming our lives and the lives of others.

CHAPTER SEVEN

THE FAVOR OF GOD IN ALL ASPECTS OF LIFE

F avor is a gift that manifests in every area of a believer's life. When we walk in divine favor, it touches not just one part of our lives, but every aspect, spiritual, financial, relational, and physical. God's favor is holistic, meaning that it is designed to permeate all areas of existence, allowing us to experience His blessings in every facet of life.

Spiritual Favor

The most foundational aspect of God's favor is spiritual favor. This is the favor that gives us access to God's presence, salvation, and spiritual growth. It is by God's grace and favor that we are drawn into a relationship with Him. Ephesians 2:8 reminds us,

> *"For by grace you have been saved through faith, and that not of yourselves; it is the gift of God."*

The gift of salvation is the ultimate manifestation of God's favor, opening the door for us to experience His love, forgiveness, and eternal life.

Spiritual favor also includes the grace to grow in our

relationship with God. This favor is reflected in the wisdom, discernment, and spiritual gifts that God bestows upon believers. When we align our hearts with God's will and pursue Him through prayer, worship, and studying His Word, we open ourselves to deeper levels of spiritual favor. This favor equips us for ministry, service, and fulfilling God's purpose in our lives.

For instance, Daniel, who was highly favored in God's sight, experienced extraordinary spiritual favor. Because of his commitment to prayer and devotion to God, he received revelations, dreams, and visions that provided guidance not only for himself but also for entire nations (Daniel 6:10-28). Daniel's spiritual favor impacted every other aspect of his life, demonstrating how deeply intertwined spiritual favor is with other areas of our lives.

Financial Favor

God's favor also manifests in our financial life. Financial favor is not simply about acquiring wealth, it is about God's provision and stewardship. It includes God opening doors for financial opportunities, blessing the work of our hands, and providing for our needs. Deuteronomy 8:18 says,

> *"And you shall remember the Lord your God, for it is He who gives you power to get wealth."*

Financial favor is the empowerment that comes from God to access resources that enable us to live abundantly and support His work.

When we experience financial favor, we often find that God places us in positions where our financial needs are met in unexpected ways. It could be through new business opportunities, promotions at work, or even miraculous provision. Joseph's life is a prime example of financial favor.

Even though he was sold into slavery, God's favor was with him, and he rose to become the second most powerful man in Egypt, managing the nation's resources during a time of famine (Genesis 41:39-41).

Joseph's financial favor not only provided for his family but also saved an entire nation from starvation. This shows that financial favor is not just about personal gain; it is a tool for advancing God's purposes and blessing others. When we are faithful stewards of the financial favor God grants us, He entrusts us with more.

Relational Favor

Relational favor is another important aspect of God's blessings in our lives. Relational favor refers to the ability to cultivate meaningful and supportive relationships. These relationships may include family, friendships, partnerships, or divine connections that align us with people who help us fulfill our purpose. Proverbs 18:22 says,

> "He who finds a wife finds a good thing, and obtains favor from the Lord."

This shows how relational favor extends even into the covenant of marriage, where God blesses and strengthens relationships.

Relational favor is seen in how God places the right people in our lives at the right time. These are individuals who mentor, support, or partner with us in our journey. The story of Ruth is a powerful example of relational favor. After the death of her husband, Ruth's loyalty to her mother-in-law, Naomi, led her to Boaz, a man of wealth and influence. Through Boaz, Ruth experienced not only personal favor but also became part of the lineage of King David, and ultimately, Jesus Christ (Ruth 2:11-12).

God's relational favor opens doors for divine connections that lead to opportunities for growth, support, and purpose. It can also manifest in reconciliation and restoration in families and friendships, showing the power of God's hand in our relationships.

Physical Favor

Physical favor includes divine health, protection, and strength. God's favor extends to our physical well-being, granting us health and vitality to carry out His work. The Bible is filled with promises of divine health and healing, showing that God cares about our bodies as much as He cares about our souls. In 3 John 1:2, the apostle John writes,

> *"Beloved, I pray that you may prosper in all things and be in health, just as your soul prospers."*

Physical favor manifests in healing from sickness, protection from harm, and supernatural strength to endure physical challenges. One notable example is found in the life of Elijah. When Elijah was physically exhausted and ready to give up, God provided him with supernatural food that gave him the strength to continue his journey for 40 days and nights (1 Kings 19:4-8).

Physical favor does not mean that we will never face health challenges or physical trials, but it assures us that God is our healer and sustainer. Through prayer and faith, we can access divine health and strength, allowing us to live out God's purpose in good physical condition.

Testimonies Of Favor Transforming Lives

Throughout history and within the Bible, we see how the

favor of God has transformed the lives of individuals, families, and even entire nations. These testimonies not only serve as powerful reminders of God's ability to work in every aspect of our lives, but they also inspire us to believe for favor in our own circumstances.

The Story Of Esther: A Life Transformed By Favor

One of the most striking testimonies of God's favor is the story of Esther, a young Jewish woman who became queen of Persia and used her position to save her people from destruction. Esther's rise to prominence was not by chance; it was orchestrated by divine favor. Although she was an orphan, raised by her cousin Mordecai, Esther was chosen by King Xerxes to be queen, a role that positioned her for an extraordinary assignment.

Esther 2:17 tells us,

> *"The king loved Esther more than all the other women, and she obtained grace and favor in his sight more than all the virgins; so he set the royal crown upon her head."*

Esther's favor was evident in her selection as queen, but it became even more significant when she had to act on behalf of her people.

When Haman, an official in the king's court, plotted to exterminate the Jewish people, Esther risked her life by approaching the king without being summoned. In (Esther 5:2), we read that the king extended his scepter to her, a symbol of his favor. As a result of Esther's courage and God's favor, the Jewish people were saved from destruction.

Esther's story shows us that favor is not just about personal advancement, it is about being in the right position to fulfill

God's purposes. Her testimony encourages us to trust in God's favor, knowing that He can use us to bring about deliverance, justice, and transformation for others.

The Testimony Of Solomon's Wisdom And Wealth

King Solomon's life is another powerful testimony of how God's favor can transform every aspect of life. Solomon's favor was evident in both spiritual and financial areas. After Solomon became king, God appeared to him in a dream and offered to grant him whatever he asked. Rather than asking for wealth or long life, Solomon asked for wisdom to govern God's people justly. Pleased with his request, God not only granted him wisdom but also promised him wealth, honor, and long life (1 Kings 3:5-14).

Solomon's wisdom became legendary, attracting leaders and nations from all over the world. His financial favor was unmatched, as the kingdom of Israel prospered under his reign. In 1 Kings 10:23-24, we read,

> *"So King Solomon surpassed all the kings of the earth in riches and wisdom. Now all the earth sought the presence of Solomon to hear his wisdom, which God had put in his heart."*

Solomon's story demonstrates how spiritual favor, in the form of wisdom, can lead to financial and relational favor. His wisdom not only brought wealth but also established Israel as a powerful nation with influential alliances. Solomon's testimony reminds us that favor is multi-dimensional, touching every part of life when we seek God first.

Modern Testimonies Of Favor

Even in modern times, we see countless testimonies of how God's favor transforms lives. Whether it's miraculous healings, unexpected financial breakthroughs, or divine connections that lead to career advancements, God's favor is still at work in the lives of believers today.

For example, a woman struggling with infertility might receive a doctor's report declaring that she will never conceive, yet after prayer and faith, she experiences God's favor in the form of a healthy pregnancy. Or a business owner facing financial ruin may suddenly receive a lucrative contract that saves their company, an event that they can only attribute to God's favor. These testimonies illustrate the truth that God's favor is not limited by time or circumstance. It is available to all who seek Him and walk in alignment with His will.

How To Sustain And Multiply Favor In Your Life

While receiving favor is a blessing, learning how to sustain and multiply it is equally important. Favor is not a one-time event; it is something that can increase and expand throughout your life when stewarded properly. I will teach you key principles that will help you sustain and multiply God's favor in every aspect of your life.

Walking In Obedience To God's Word:

The foundation for sustaining and multiplying favor is obedience to God's word. Just as obedience attracts favor, continued obedience ensures that we remain in a position to receive and increase in favor. In Deuteronomy 28:1-2, God promises,

> *"Now it shall come to pass, if you diligently obey the voice of the Lord your God, to observe carefully all His commandments... the Lord your God will set you high*

above all nations of the earth. And all these blessings shall come upon you and overtake you, because you obey the voice of the Lord your God."

Obedience is not just about following rules, it is about aligning our lives with God's principles. When we live according to God's Word, we create an environment where favor can flourish. This includes being faithful in the small things, maintaining integrity, and walking in love and forgiveness toward others.

Cultivating Gratitude and Humility:

Gratitude and humility are essential for sustaining favor. When we remain humble and thankful for the blessings we receive, we create a posture of heart that attracts more favor. Gratitude acknowledges that every good gift comes from God (James 1:17), while humility keeps us from becoming prideful or self-reliant.

King Solomon, though favored with great wisdom and wealth, demonstrated the importance of humility early in his reign. In 1 Kings 3:7, Solomon acknowledges,

"Now, O Lord my God, You have made Your servant king instead of my father David, but I am a little child; I do not know how to go out or come in."

His humility and dependence on God positioned him for the incredible favor he later experienced.

Stewardship And Generosity:

Sustaining and multiplying favor requires good stewardship of what we have been given. This means managing our resources, time, and relationships wisely. Jesus taught that those who are faithful with little will be entrusted with more (Luke 16:10). Stewardship also includes being generous with what God has blessed us with. When we give generously, we position ourselves to receive even greater favor in return.

In 2 Corinthians 9:6-8, Paul writes,

> *"He who sows sparingly will also reap sparingly, and he who sows bountifully will also reap bountifully... And God is able to make all grace abound toward you, that you, always having all sufficiency in all things, may have an abundance for every good work."*

Generosity unlocks greater levels of favor because it reflects God's heart and aligns us with His purposes.

Maintaining A Prayerful Life:

Prayer is vital to sustaining and multiplying favor. We remain connected to God through prayer, seeking His guidance, protection, and blessings. Regular communication with God keeps us sensitive to His leading and allows us to align our desires with His will.

Daniel's life exemplifies the power of a prayerful life. Even after receiving favor in the courts of Babylon, Daniel continued his daily practice of prayer, seeking God's wisdom and direction (Daniel 6:10). His consistent prayer life ensured that he remained in a position of favor, even when faced with adversity.

Walking In Faith And Expectation:

Finally, sustaining and multiplying favor requires walking in faith and maintaining an expectation of God's goodness. Hebrews 11:6 reminds us that *"without faith, it is impossible to please Him, for he who comes to God must believe that He is and that He is a rewarder of those who diligently seek Him."*

Faith keeps us anchored in God's promises, while expectation positions us to receive.

When we expect favor, we align our thoughts, actions, and prayers with God's will. This expectation draws favor into our lives because it reflects a heart that trusts in God's goodness and provision.

The favor of God is not limited to one area of our lives, it is comprehensive and touches every part of who we are, spiritually, financially, relationally, and physically. Through the examples of biblical figures like Esther, Solomon, and modern testimonies, we see that God's favor transforms lives and opens doors that no one can shut.

To sustain and multiply this favor, we must walk in obedience, cultivate humility, steward our blessings well, maintain a life of prayer, and live with faith and expectation. God desires to pour out His favor on His children, and when we align our lives with His will, we can experience the fullness of His blessings in every aspect of our lives.

CHAPTER EIGHT

WALKING IN A LIFETIME OF UNLIMITED FAVOR

◆ ◆ ◆

Building a Lasting Legacy
Through Favor

F avor is not just a temporary blessing; it is meant to be sustained and multiplied over time, leaving a lasting legacy. Walking in a lifetime of unlimited favor requires intentionality, commitment, and a deep understanding of how favor operates. It is about living in a way that not only attracts favor but also ensures that this favor has a long-term impact on your life and those who come after you.

A legacy is passed down from one generation to the next. When we think of leaving a legacy, we often think of wealth, reputation, or influence. However, a legacy built through favor goes beyond material possessions or social standing. It is about leaving a spiritual and moral inheritance that reflects God's goodness and favor in every area of life.

Legacy through favor is seen in the lives of biblical figures like Abraham, David, and Solomon, who left behind not just wealth and kingdoms but a lasting spiritual legacy. For example, God's promise to Abraham was not limited to his lifetime but extended to his descendants. In Genesis 17:7, God says,

> *"And I will establish My covenant between Me and you and your descendants after you in their generations, for an everlasting covenant, to be God to you and your descendants after you." Abraham's obedience and faith secured favor for generations, making him the father of many nations.*

Leaving a lasting legacy through favor means living so that God's blessings continue to flow through future generations. It involves making decisions that reflect God's will, building relationships rooted in His principles, and having a heart of humility and obedience.

Favor Beyond Personal Success

Building a legacy of favor is not just about personal success or achievement; it is about using the favor God gives us to bless others and further His kingdom. When we walk in favor, we are positioned to make an impact beyond our lives. This is why legacy is so important in the context of favor. It ensures that the blessings we receive are not just for our benefit but for the benefit of others.

One of the most potent examples of this is seen in the life of King David. David was a man after God's own heart, and throughout his life, he experienced favor in many areas, military victories, leadership, and personal devotion to God. However, David's legacy went beyond his reign. His favor with God extended to his son, Solomon, and ultimately to the Messiah, Jesus Christ, who came from David's lineage.

David's commitment to building a lasting legacy is evident in his preparations for the temple's construction. Although God did not allow David to build the temple himself, he made extensive preparations to ensure that his son Solomon would have everything needed to complete the task. In 1 Chronicles 22:5, David says,

> *"My son Solomon is young and inexperienced, and the house to be built for the Lord must be exceedingly magnificent, famous and glorious throughout all countries. I will now make preparations for it."*

David's vision extended beyond his lifetime, ensuring that his legacy of favor would continue through Solomon.

Stewarding Favor To Leave A Mark

To build a lasting legacy through favor, it is essential to steward favor well. Stewardship involves managing the resources, opportunities, and blessings God entrusts us. When we are faithful stewards of the favor we receive, we increase it and ensure that it has a lasting impact.

The parable of the talents in (Matthew 25:14-30) illustrates the importance of stewardship. In the parable, a master gives his servants different amounts of money (talents) and expects them to invest and multiply what they have been given. The servant who wisely invests and multiplies his talents is rewarded even more, while the servant who buried his talent in the ground loses everything. This parable teaches us that favor, like talents, must be used wisely and multiplied. If we fail to steward favor, we risk losing it altogether.

Building a legacy through favor requires us to recognize that the blessings we receive are not just for our benefit but for the greater good. By using favor to serve others, advance God's kingdom, and bless future generations, we ensure that our legacy of favor endures.

Transgenerational Favor:

Leaving a Mark for Generations to Come. Favor is not limited to a single lifetime; it can extend to future generations. Transgenerational favor refers to the blessings and favors that flow from one generation to the next. This type of favor is often a result of the faithfulness, obedience, and commitment of one individual whose actions create a ripple effect of blessings for their descendants. Transgenerational favor is a recurring theme in Scripture, where God's blessings on one individual or family extend far beyond their lifetime. This is particularly evident in the covenant promises God made with Abraham, which continued through Isaac, Jacob, and the nation of Israel. In Genesis 22:17, God promises Abraham,

> *"I will bless you and multiply your descendants as the stars of heaven and as the sand which is on the seashore; and your descendants shall possess the gate of their enemies."*

Abraham's faith and obedience laid the foundation for generations of favor. His willingness to sacrifice his son Isaac in obedience to God secured a blessing that extended to all his descendants. This shows us that our decisions today can impact future generations, either positively or negatively.

The Story Of Ruth And Boaz: A Legacy Of Favor

The story of Ruth and Boaz is another powerful example of how transgenerational favor operates. Ruth, a Moabite widow, aligned herself with the God of Israel and demonstrated loyalty and humility by staying with her mother-in-law, Naomi. Despite her difficult circumstances, Ruth's faithfulness and humble heart positioned her for a favor. Through her marriage to Boaz, a man of wealth and influence, Ruth became part of the lineage of King David and, ultimately, Jesus Christ.

Ruth's story teaches us that even when we start from a disadvantage or hardship, favor can elevate us and create a legacy for future generations. Her decision to follow Naomi and embrace the God of Israel changed her life and set the stage for her descendants to walk in divine favor.

Ruth and Boaz's legacy continued through their son, Obed, who became the father of Jesse, the father of King David. This transgenerational favor culminated in the birth of Jesus, the Messiah. Ruth's humble and faithful heart created a ripple effect that impacted her family and the entire world.

The Importance Of Generational Blessings

The Bible extensively discusses the importance of generational blessings and curses. Exodus 20:6 says that God shows mercy and favor

> "to thousands, to those who love Me and keep My commandments."

This verse signifies that our obedience to God secures favor for us and future generations.

One of the most striking examples of generational favor is found in the life of King Solomon. Solomon's favor with God was partly a result of the covenant God made with his father, David. Even when Solomon strayed from God's commandments later in his life, God's favor in his kingdom remained because of His promise to David. In 1 Kings 11:12-13, God says,

"Nevertheless, I will not do it in your days, for the sake of your father David; but I will tear it out of the hand of your son. However, I will not tear away the whole kingdom; I will give one tribe to your son for the sake of My servant David."

This passage demonstrates how transgenerational favor works. David's obedience and devotion to God secured favor for his descendants, even when they did not fully walk in God's ways. This teaches us the powerful truth that the favor we experience can have a lasting impact on future generations.

How To Secure Transgenerational Favor

Securing transgenerational favor requires a commitment to live in alignment with God's will. The choices we make, the values we uphold, and the faith we demonstrate all contribute to the legacy we leave behind. To secure transgenerational favor, we must:

- **Walk in Obedience**: Just as Abraham, David, and Ruth demonstrated, obedience to God is foundational for securing favor that lasts beyond our lifetime. Our faithfulness today sets the stage for future generations to experience God's blessings.

- **Having Faith and Trust in God**: Transgenerational favor often flows through families that maintain a deep faith in God. Passing on the knowledge of God, His promises, and His faithfulness to future generations ensures that they continue to walk in His favor.

- **Leave a Spiritual Inheritance**: While material wealth can be passed down from generation to generation, a spiritual inheritance is far more valuable. Teaching future generations about God's word, prayer, and a life of obedience leaves them equipped to walk in God's favor.

The Role Of Prayer And Commitment In Maintaining Favor Over Time

Walking in a lifetime of unlimited favor requires more than just receiving God's blessings; it requires a deep commitment to maintaining favor over time. Prayer and dedication to God's will play crucial roles in ensuring that the favor we receive continues to grow and multiply throughout our lives.

• The Power of Prayer in Sustaining Favor

Prayer is one of the most important ways to maintain and grow in favor. Through prayer, we remain connected to God and aligned with His purposes. Prayer keeps us sensitive to the Holy Spirit's leading and allows us to seek God's wisdom and guidance in every area of our lives.

In the life of Daniel, we see how prayer played a pivotal role in maintaining favor. Daniel experienced favor in the Babylonian courts, rising to a position of influence under multiple kings. Despite the pressures and challenges, he faced, Daniel remained committed to prayer. In (Daniel 6:10), we read that Daniel prayed three times a day, even when it was forbidden by law. His faithfulness in prayer not only sustained his favor but also led to miraculous deliverance when he was thrown into the lion's den.

Daniel's life teaches us that prayer is essential for sustaining favor over time. When we maintain a strong prayer life, we stay connected to God's power and provision, allowing us to navigate challenges and continue to experience His favor.

• Commitment to God's Will and Purpose

In addition to prayer, maintaining favor requires a steadfast commitment to God's will and purpose. Walking in favor is not about pursuing our own desires but about aligning ourselves with God's plan for our lives. When we commit to God's will, we create an environment where favor can flourish.

In the New Testament, we see this principle in the life of Apostle Paul. Paul's commitment to preaching the Gospel, despite persecution and hardship, ensured that God's favor remained on his ministry. Even when Paul faced imprisonment and suffering, God's favor opened doors for him to continue his work. In (Acts 16), Paul and Silas were thrown into prison, but through their prayers and worship, God caused an earthquake that opened the prison doors, leading to the conversion of the jailer and his family (Acts 16:25-34).

Paul's unwavering commitment to God's purpose allowed him to walk in continuous favor, even in difficult circumstances. His life shows us that favor is not about avoiding challenges but about experiencing God's provision and grace in the midst of them.

• Faithfulness in the Small Things

To maintain favor over time, it is important to be faithful to the small things. Jesus taught in Luke 16:10,

"He who is faithful in what is least is faithful also in much."

This principle applies to how we handle the favor we receive. When we are faithful with the blessings and opportunities God gives us, we position ourselves for even greater favor.

Faithfulness involves stewarding our time, resources, and relationships with integrity and care. It means showing up consistently, even when no one is watching, and making choices that honor God. When we demonstrate faithfulness in the small things, God can trust us with greater responsibilities and blessings.

• Trusting in God's Timing

Lastly, maintaining favor requires trusting in God's timing. Favor does not always manifest immediately, and there may be seasons of waiting or challenges that test our faith. However, trusting in God's timing ensures that we remain patient and faithful, knowing that His plans are perfect.

In the story of Joseph, we see how God's favor unfolded over time. After being sold into slavery and imprisoned, Joseph could have given up hope. However, he remained faithful to God, trusting in His timing. Eventually, Joseph was elevated to a position of great influence in Egypt, where he saved many lives during a famine (Genesis 41:39-40).

Joseph's story teaches us that even when favor seems delayed, God is working behind the scenes to bring about His purposes. Trusting in God's timing allows us to walk in a lifetime of favor, knowing He will fulfill His promises in due time.

Walking in a lifetime of unlimited favor is about more than just experiencing blessings, it is about building a legacy that lasts through the generations and transgenerational favor, we can leave a mark that impacts not only our own lives but the lives of those who come after us.

Prayer and commitment are essential to maintaining and multiplying favor over time. As we remain faithful to God's will and trust in His timing, we can walk in a lifetime of unlimited favor, knowing that His blessings will continue to flow throughout our lives and beyond.

CHAPTER NINE

THE FOUNDATION
OF FAVOR THROUGH
RIGHTEOUSNESS

◆ ◆ ◆

The Link Between
Righteousness and Favor

T he connection between righteousness and favor is one of the most foundational principles in Scripture. Righteousness is a state of being in right standing with God, and it is essential for experiencing the fullness of His favor. But what does it mean to be righteous, and how does righteousness attract favor?

At its core, righteousness is about being aligned with God's will and character. It involves living a life that reflects God's holiness, love, and justice. Righteousness is not merely about following a set of rules; it is about having a heart that desires to please God. This heart posture attracts God's favor, as He delights in those who walk in righteousness.

Psalm 5:12 tells us,

"For You, O Lord, will bless the righteous; with favor You will surround him as with a shield."

This verse illustrates how God surrounds the righteous with His favor, protecting and blessing them in every area of life. The image of favor as a shield is significant because it suggests that favor not only brings blessings but also guards us from harm. This protective aspect of favor directly results from living a life of righteousness.

The Blessings Of Righteousness

The blessings that come from walking in righteousness are multifaceted. Righteousness brings spiritual, physical, financial, and relational blessings, all of which are manifestations of God's favor.

- **Spiritual Favor**: The most important blessing of righteousness is the spiritual favor we receive. This includes a close relationship with God, access to His presence, and the indwelling of the Holy Spirit. Righteousness allows us to walk intimately with God, experiencing His guidance, wisdom, and comfort in every situation.

- **Physical Favor**: Righteousness also brings physical blessings. Proverbs 3:7-8 says,

  "Do not be wise in your own eyes; fear the Lord and depart from evil. It will be health to your flesh and strength to your bones."

  This passage highlights the physical health and vitality that comes from living in righteousness. When we live according to God's principles, we avoid many of the physical and emotional stresses that come from sinful living.

- **Financial Favor**: Righteousness positions us to receive God's provision and financial blessings. Proverbs 10:6 says, "Blessings are on the head of the righteous." These blessings include financial prosperity, as God entrusts resources to those who are faithful stewards of His wealth.

- **Relational Favor**: Finally, righteousness brings relational favor. Proverbs 3:3-4 says,

"Let not mercy and truth forsake you; bind them around your neck, write them on the tablet of your heart, and so find favor and high esteem in the sight of God and man."

Righteousness cultivates healthy, God honoring relationships, as others are drawn to the integrity and kindness that flow from a righteous life.

Righteousness As A Covenant Relationship

Righteousness is not something we achieve by our own efforts. It is a result of the covenant relationship we have with God through Jesus Christ. In the Old Testament, righteousness was often linked to obedience to the Law. However, under the New Covenant, righteousness is given to us through faith in Jesus Christ.

2 Corinthians 5:21 explains,

"For He made Him who knew no sin to be sin for us, that we might become the righteousness of God in Him."

This verse signifies the incredible exchange that took place on the cross. Jesus took on our sin so that we could be made righteous in Him. This righteousness is a gift of grace, and it is the foundation of the favor we experience as believers.

While we are made righteous through Christ, we are also called to walk in righteousness. This means living in a way that reflects the righteousness we have received. Our actions, thoughts, and words should align with God's character, and as we do so, we open ourselves to greater levels of favor.

Biblical Examples Of Righteousness And Favor

The Bible is filled with examples of individuals who walked in righteousness and experienced God's favor as a result. These stories serve as powerful reminders of the blessings that flow from living a righteous life.

Noah: Righteousness In The Midst Of A Wicked Generation

One of the most striking examples of righteousness leading to favor is the story of Noah. Noah lived in a time when the world was filled with wickedness and violence. Genesis 6:5 describes the state of humanity: "Then the Lord saw that the wickedness of man was great in the earth, and that every intent of the thoughts of his heart was only evil continually."

Despite the widespread corruption, Noah found favor in God's eyes because he was righteous. Genesis 6:8-9 says,

> *"But Noah found grace (favor) in the eyes of the Lord. This is the genealogy of Noah. Noah was a just man, perfect in his generations. Noah walked with God."*

Noah's righteousness set him apart from the rest of the world, and as a result, God extended His favor to Noah and his family.

Noah's favor was not just a personal blessing, it had a generational impact. Because of Noah's righteousness, God chose to spare him and his family from the flood that destroyed the rest of the earth. This story illustrates how righteousness not only brings personal favor but also protects and blesses those connected to us.

Job: Righteousness In The Face Of Suffering

The story of Job is another powerful example of righteousness leading to favor. Job was described as *"blameless and upright, and one who feared God and shunned evil"* (Job 1:1). Because of his righteousness, Job enjoyed great favor in every area of his life. He was blessed with wealth, health, and a large family.

However, Job's righteousness was tested when he lost everything his wealth, his children, and his health. Despite his immense suffering, Job remained committed to righteousness. In Job 1:21, he declares,

> *"The Lord gave, and the Lord has taken away; blessed be the name of the Lord."*

Job's faithfulness in the face of suffering ultimately led to a restoration of favor. Job 42:10 tells us,

> *"And the Lord restored Job's losses when he prayed for his friends. Indeed, the Lord gave Job twice as much as he had before."*

Job's story teaches us that righteousness is not dependent on our circumstances. Even when we face trials, we must remain committed to living a righteous life. When we do, God's favor will ultimately be restored, often in greater measure than before.

Joseph: Righteousness And Integrity In Adversity

Joseph is another example of how righteousness and integrity attract favor, even in the midst of adversity. As a young man, Joseph was sold into slavery by his own brothers, yet he remained faithful to God. Despite the injustice he faced, Joseph consistently walked in righteousness, refusing to compromise his integrity.

One of the most significant tests of Joseph's righteousness came when he was falsely accused of attempting to seduce Potiphar's wife. Instead of giving in to temptation, Joseph remained righteous, saying, *"How then can I do this great wickedness, and sin against God?"* (Genesis 39:9). Although Joseph was imprisoned as a result of the false accusation, his righteousness ultimately led to God's favor being poured out in his life.

Genesis 39:21 says,

> *"But the Lord was with Joseph and showed him mercy, and He gave him favor in the sight of the keeper of the prison."*

Joseph's righteousness continued to attract God's favor, even in prison. Eventually, this favor led to his promotion as the second-in-command in Egypt, where he was used by God to save many lives during a famine.

Joseph's story demonstrates that righteousness does not always lead to immediate blessings. Sometimes, walking in righteousness may result in temporary setbacks or challenges. However, as we remain faithful, God's favor will ultimately bring restoration and elevation.

Righteousness In Our Daily Lives

The examples of Noah, Job, and Joseph show us the power of righteousness in attracting favor. But how do we apply this principle in our daily lives? Walking in righteousness requires intentionality and commitment. It is about making choices that honor God, even in the small things.

Righteousness In Our Thoughts

Righteousness is not just about our outward actions or the things we do; it begins in the heart and manifests through our thoughts. The Bible teaches us that God looks at the heart (1 Samuel 16:7), including our inner thoughts, motives, and attitudes. Our thought life is crucial in determining whether we walk in righteousness or fall into sin. To experience God's favor, developing righteous thinking that aligns with His will and His word is vital.

The mind is often described as the battlefield where spiritual warfare takes place. In 2 Corinthians 10:4-5, Paul writes,

> *"For the weapons of our warfare are not carnal but mighty in God for pulling down strongholds, casting down arguments and every high thing that exalts itself against the knowledge of God, bringing every thought into captivity to the obedience of Christ."*

This scripture signifies the importance of taking control of our thoughts and ensuring they are submitted to Christ. Failure to do so allows ungodly thoughts to become strongholds, influencing our behavior and leading us away from righteousness.

Righteousness in our thoughts begins with recognizing that our mind is the battleground for spiritual victory. Every day, we are bombarded with thoughts, some from God, some from the enemy, and some from our flesh. Unrighteous thoughts can take root and lead to sin if we are not vigilant. James 1:14-15 explains this process: *"But each one is tempted when he is drawn away by his desires and enticed. Then, when desire has conceived, it gives birth to sin; when it is full-grown, sin brings forth death."* The journey from temptation to sin begins in the mind, so cultivating righteousness in our thoughts is crucial.

Righteousness in our thoughts means aligning our thinking with God's word. Scripture is the foundation for righteous living, including our inner thought life. Philippians 4:8 provides a clear guideline for how we should direct our thoughts,

> *"Finally, brethren, whatever things are true, whatever things are noble, whatever things are just, whatever things are pure, whatever things are lovely, whatever things are of good report, if there is any virtue and if there is anything praiseworthy, meditate on these things."*

This verse encourages us to focus on thoughts that are consistent with God's character and standards, thinking on things that are true, noble, just, and pure sets the tone for righteousness in our entire being. When we meditate on God's goodness, promises, and truths, our minds align with His will, and we are better equipped to make decisions that reflect righteousness.

Jesus Himself emphasized the importance of our thoughts in His teachings. In Matthew 5:27-28, He said,

> *"You have heard that it was said to those of old, 'You shall not commit adultery.' But I say to you that whoever looks at a woman to lust for her has already committed*

adultery with her in his heart."

Here, Jesus addresses the reality that sin begins in the mind. Even if outwardly, we appear righteous, God is concerned with the purity of our inner thoughts.

We must actively guard our minds to walk in righteousness in our thoughts. Proverbs 4:23 instructs us,

> *"Above all else, guard your heart, for everything you do flows from it."*

The heart and mind are deeply connected, and the thoughts we allow into our minds will ultimately shape our character and actions. Therefore, we must be intentional about what we expose ourselves to, whether through media, conversations, or other influences.

One practical way to guard our minds is through the process of renewing them. Romans 12:2 tells us,

> *"Do not be conformed to this world, but be transformed by the renewing of your mind, that you may prove what is that good and acceptable and perfect will of God."*

Renewing our minds involves replacing worldly or ungodly thoughts with the truth of God's word. This ongoing transformation requires consistent engagement with Scripture, prayer, and reflection on God's promises.

Guarding our minds also involves filtering out negative or harmful thoughts. Not every thought that enters our mind comes from God. The enemy often tries to plant seeds of doubt, fear, and temptation, hoping that these thoughts will grow and lead to unrighteous actions. 1 Peter 5:8 warns us to

> *"be sober, be vigilant; because your adversary the devil walks about like a roaring lion, seeking whom he may devour."*

We must be sober-minded and alert, discerning the source of our thoughts and rejecting anything that does not align with God's truth.

Another key aspect of developing righteousness in our thoughts is the power of confession. When we recognize that our thoughts are not aligned with God's word, we can confess them to God and ask for His help to redirect our thinking. 1 John 1:9 assures us,

> *"If we confess our sins, He is faithful and just to forgive us our sins and to cleanse us from all unrighteousness."*

This includes unrighteous thoughts. God is gracious to cleanse us and help us when we bring our struggles to Him.

Managing our thoughts is not just about resisting negative influences, it also involves filling our minds with the right things. Colossians 3:2 tells us,

> *"Set your mind on things above, not on things on the earth."*

When we intentionally focus on heavenly things, on God's kingdom, His righteousness, His purposes, we create an environment in our mind that is conducive to righteous living.

We can also manage our thoughts by engaging in spiritual

disciplines like meditation on Scripture, prayer, and worship. These practices help to center our minds on God's presence and His promises. Psalm 1:2-3 describes the blessed person whose

> *"delight is in the law of the Lord, and in His law he meditates day and night. He shall be like a tree planted by the rivers of water, that brings forth its fruit in its season, whose leaf also shall not wither; and whatever he does shall prosper."*

Meditation on God's word helps our minds to stay fixed on righteousness and positions us to bear spiritual fruit.

Righteousness In Our Speech

Our words carry immense power. Scripture teaches us that the tongue has the ability to build up or tear down, to bless or curse (Proverbs 18:21). For a believer, righteousness in speech is essential because our words reveal the condition of our heart. Jesus emphasized this truth in Matthew 12:34 when He said,

> *"For out of the abundance of the heart the mouth speaks."*

What we say reflects what is inside us, and righteous speech is an indication of a heart that is aligned with God's will.

One of the key components of righteous speech is the ability to guard our words. (James 3:5-6) compares the tongue to a small spark that can set an entire forest on fire, highlighting the potential damage that unrighteous speech can cause. Careless words can lead to misunderstandings, hurt feelings, and broken relationships, all of which hinder the flow of God's favor in our lives. Therefore, we must be intentional about guarding our words and ensuring that what comes out of our mouths reflects the righteousness of God.

In Psalm 141:3, David prayed,

> *"Set a guard, O Lord, over my mouth; keep watch over the door of my lips."*

This prayer acknowledges that we need God's help to control our speech. Righteousness in our speech requires vigilance and discipline, as well as a heart that is sensitive to the prompting of the Holy Spirit. When we feel tempted to speak in anger, gossip, or judgment, we must ask the Holy Spirit to intervene, helping us to respond in a way that reflects God's love and truth.

Ephesians 4:29 provides a clear standard for righteous speech,

> *"Let no corrupt word proceed out of your mouth, but what is good for necessary edification, that it may impart grace to the hearers."*

Righteous speech builds up and encourages others. It seeks to bless rather than to criticize or tear down. Every conversation presents an opportunity to impart grace and wisdom, and when we speak in a way that reflects righteousness, we participate in the work of edification.

When we speak words that edify, we align our speech with the purpose of blessing others. This not only benefits those who hear but also brings favor into our lives. Proverbs 12:18 tells us,

> *"There is one who speaks like the piercings of a sword, but the tongue of the wise promotes health."*

A righteous person uses their speech to bring healing and

restoration, ensuring relationships that are marked by peace and understanding.

Righteousness in speech also means avoiding gossip, lies, slander, and negative speech. These forms of unrighteous communication can quickly damage reputations and relationships, and they are strongly condemned in Scripture. Proverbs 16:28 says,

> *"A perverse man sow's strife, and a whisperer separates the best of friends."*

Gossip and slander are tools the enemy uses to sow division, and those who engage in such behavior are walking in unrighteousness. The Bible also warns against lying and deceitful speech. Colossians 3:9 says,

> *"Do not lie to one another, since you have put off the old man with his deeds."*

As believers, we are called to walk in truth, and our words must reflect that commitment. A life of integrity means that what we say aligns with the truth of God's word. When our words are filled with truth and honesty, we build trust, strengthen relationships, and position ourselves to receive God's favor.

Lastly, righteousness in our speech involves the conscious decision to speak life and blessing over ourselves and others. In James 3:9-10, we are reminded of the inconsistency of using our tongues to both bless and curse,

"With it we bless our God and Father, and with it we curse men, who have been made in the similitude of God. Out of the same mouth proceed blessing and cursing. My brethren, these things ought not to be so." As followers of Christ, our speech should reflect a heart

of blessing, speaking life, encouragement, and truth in every situation.

Speaking life is not only about avoiding negative or harmful words but actively choosing to declare God's promises over our lives and the lives of others. When we declare God's word, we align our speech with His will, and we invite His favor into our circumstances. Proverbs 15:4 says,

> *"A wholesome tongue is a tree of life, but perverseness in it breaks the spirit."*

By cultivating righteousness in our speech, we foster an environment of life, peace, and favor.

Righteousness In Our Actions

While righteousness in our speech is crucial, it must be matched by righteousness in our actions. The Bible makes it clear that true righteousness is not just about what we say but about how we live. Our actions are the outward expression of our faith, and they serve as a testimony to the world of our relationship with God. Jesus said in Matthew 5:16,

> *"Let your light so shine before men, that they may see your good works and glorify your Father in heaven."*

Righteous actions are a reflection of God's character and an invitation for others to experience His goodness.

Integrity is the foundation of righteous actions. Proverbs 10:9 says,

> *"He who walks with integrity walks securely, but he who perverts his ways will become known."*

Integrity means that our actions align with God's standards, even when no one is watching. It is a commitment to doing what is right, regardless of the consequences or external pressures. When we live with integrity, we build trust, foster healthy relationships, and position ourselves to receive God's favor.

Righteousness in our actions means consistently striving to honor God. Whether in our personal lives, our workplaces, or our communities, our actions should reflect the righteousness of Christ. This includes how we handle our finances, how we treat others, and how we respond to challenges. Integrity requires consistency in every area of life, not just when it's convenient or advantageous.

Righteousness in our actions also involves showing compassion and generosity to those in need. Throughout Scripture, God commands His people to care for the poor, the widow, the orphan, and the stranger. In Isaiah 58:6-7, God speaks through the prophet, saying,

> *"Is this not the fast that I have chosen: to loose the bonds of wickedness, to undo the heavy burdens, to let the oppressed go free, and that you break every yoke? Is it not to share your bread with the hungry, and that you bring the poor who are cast out to your house?"*

True righteousness is demonstrated in how we serve others and extend God's love through practical acts of kindness. Jesus Himself modeled this throughout His ministry, healing the sick, feeding the hungry, and offering compassion to the marginalized. Righteous actions are rooted in a heart of love, seeking to uplift others and meet their needs.

When we are generous with our time, resources, and love, we reflect God's heart and position ourselves to receive more of His blessings. Proverbs 11:25 reminds us,

> *"The generous soul will be made rich, and he who waters will also be watered himself."*

Generosity is a key aspect of righteous living, and it opens the door for God's favor to flow into every area of our lives.

James 2:17 tells us,

> *"faith by itself, if it does not have works, is dead."*

Righteousness in our actions means that our faith must be active, demonstrated through our choices and how we live. Faith without corresponding action is incomplete. It's not enough to profess belief in God; our actions must reflect our trust in Him.

Abraham is a powerful example of this principle. When God called him to leave his homeland and journey to a place that He would show him, Abraham obeyed, even though he did not know the destination. His faith was made complete through his actions. James 2:22 says,
"Do you see that faith was working together with his works, and by works faith was made perfect?"

Abraham's actions demonstrated his faith, so he experienced God's favor and blessing.

Living righteously means taking steps of faith, even when we do not see the whole picture. It means trusting God enough to act on His word in small daily decisions or life-altering moments. When we align our actions with God's will, we position ourselves for divine favor and breakthrough.

Obedience is at the heart of righteous actions. In 1 Samuel 15:22, Samuel tells Saul,

"Has the Lord as great delight in burnt offerings and sacrifices, as in obeying the voice of the Lord? Behold, to obey is better than sacrifice."

God values obedience above all else because it reflects a heart surrendered to His will. Obedience is the pathway to God's favor, and when we walk in obedience, we experience His blessings in every area of our lives.

Righteousness in our actions means saying *"yes"* to God, even when difficult or inconvenient. It involves submitting our will to His and trusting that His plans are better than ours. Like Jesus in the Garden of Gethsemane, we must learn to say, *"Not my will, but Yours be done"* (Luke 22:42). When we live in obedience, we open the door for God's favor to flow freely.

As we strive to embody righteousness in our speech and actions, we not only position ourselves to receive God's favor but also become vessels of His love and grace to those around us. Living righteously is not just about personal blessings; it is about being a light in the world, pointing others to the goodness and faithfulness of our Heavenly Father.

Maintaining A Heart Of Righteousness

Maintaining a heart of righteousness requires ongoing spiritual discipline. Just as a garden must be tended to prevent weeds from taking over, our hearts must be continually cultivated to remain righteous. This involves regular prayer, repentance, and accountability.

The Role Of Prayer In Righteousness

Prayer is essential for maintaining righteousness because it keeps us connected to God's heart and will. Through prayer, we receive the strength and guidance to live according to God's standards. Psalm 51:10-12 offers a powerful prayer for righteousness,

> *"Create a clean heart, O God, and renew a steadfast spirit within me. Do not cast me away from Your presence or take Your Holy Spirit from me. Restore the joy of Your salvation, and uphold me by Your generous Spirit."*

By prioritizing prayer daily, we ensure that our hearts remain aligned with God's will, positioning us to receive ongoing favor.

The Importance Of Repentance

Righteousness is not about perfection; it is about a heart that is quick to repent when we fall short. 1 John 1:9 assures us,

> *"If we confess our sins, He is faithful and just to forgive us our sins and to cleanse us from all unrighteousness."*

Regular repentance keeps us in the right standing with God and restores the favor that sin may block.

Repentance should be a regular part of our spiritual practice, not something we reserve for significant transgressions. By regularly examining our hearts and confessing any areas where we have failed, we ensure that nothing stands in the way of God's favor.

Accountability In Righteousness

Finally, maintaining righteousness requires accountability. Proverbs 27:17 says,

"As iron sharpens iron, so a man sharpens the countenance of his friend."

Surrounding ourselves with other believers committed to righteousness helps us stay on track and avoid the pitfalls of sin.

Accountability can be through regular fellowship, mentorship, or small group Bible studies. When we invite others to speak into our lives and hold us accountable, we strengthen our commitment to walking in righteousness and experiencing God's favor.

In conclusion, righteousness is the foundation for walking in divine favor. It is a lifestyle that reflects God's character and aligns us with His will. Through biblical examples like Noah, Job, and Joseph, we see that righteousness attracts favor and sustains it through trials and adversity.

As we commit to living righteously in our thoughts, words, and actions, we position ourselves to experience God's favor in every area of life. By maintaining a heart of righteousness through prayer, repentance, and accountability, we ensure that God's favor continues to flow, blessing us and those around us.

CHAPTER TEN

ACTIVATING FAVOR THROUGH SACRIFICIAL GIVING

◆ ◆ ◆

The Principle of Sacrificial Giving

One of the most potent keys to activating divine favor is sacrificial giving. Throughout the Bible, we see that sacrificial giving moves God's heart and opens the door for extraordinary blessings. Sacrificial giving is not just about the amount we give but the heart behind the gift. It is giving beyond what is convenient or comfortable, trusting that God will provide and bless us in return.

What Is Sacrificial Giving?

Sacrificial giving means offering something valuable to God that requires faith and trust. It goes beyond regular tithes and offerings; it is giving that stretches us and places a demand on our faith. Jesus highlighted the heart of sacrificial giving in Luke 21:1-4 when He observed a poor widow giving two small coins in the temple offering. Jesus said,

> *"Truly I tell you, this poor widow has put in more than all the others. All these people gave their gifts out of their wealth, but she, out of her poverty, put in all she had to live on."*

The widow's offering was small in monetary value but significant in sacrifice and faith. She gave out of her need, trusting that God would provide for her. This is the essence of sacrificial giving: not the amount that matters but the heart of trust and devotion accompanying the gift.

Sacrificial Giving As A Reflection Of Faith

Sacrificial giving is a profound expression of faith. When we give sacrificially, we acknowledge that God is our ultimate provider and trust Him to meet our needs. Hebrews 11:6 reminds us that

> *"without faith, it is impossible to please God."*

Sacrificial giving pleases God because it demonstrates our reliance on Him rather than on our own resources.

This principle is evident in the story of Abraham and Isaac. God asked Abraham to sacrifice his only son, Isaac, the son through whom God had promised to bless Abraham's descendants (Genesis 22:1-18). This request required Abraham to exercise incredible faith. Abraham obeyed despite the cost, trusting that God could raise Isaac from the dead if necessary (Hebrews 11:19).

Abraham's sacrificial obedience extraordinarily activated God's favor. Because of his willingness to give what was most precious to him, God blessed Abraham and his descendants with generational favor. Genesis 22:16-17 records God's response to Abraham's sacrifice,

> *"By Myself, I have sworn, says the Lord because you have done this thing and have not withheld your son, your only son, blessing I will bless you, and multiplying I will multiply your descendants as the stars of the heaven and as the sand which is on the seashore."*

Abraham's sacrificial giving impacted his life and secured favor for future generations. This demonstrates that sacrificial giving can unlock immediate blessings and long-term, generational favor.

Biblical Examples Of Sacrificial Giving

Throughout Scripture, we find numerous examples of individuals who activated divine favor through sacrificial giving. These stories reveal that giving sacrificially opens us to supernatural provision, breakthrough, and favor.

The Widow Of Zarephath: A Miracle Of Provision

One of the most striking examples of sacrificial giving is found in the story of the widow of Zarephath. During a severe famine, the prophet Elijah was sent to the town of Zarephath, where he encountered a widow preparing her last meal for herself and her son. She had only a handful of flour and a little oil left, and she expected that after this meal, they would starve to death.

Despite her desperate situation, Elijah asked her to make him a small cake before preparing food for herself and her son. Elijah assured her that if she obeyed, the flour and oil would not run out until the famine was over. In 1 Kings 17:13-14, Elijah says,

> *"Do not fear; go and do as you have said, but make me a small cake from it first, and bring it to me; and afterward make some for yourself and your son. For thus says the Lord God of Israel: 'The bin of flour shall not be used up, nor shall the jar of oil run dry, until the day the Lord sends rain on the earth.'"*

The widow's response required incredible faith. She gave sacrificially out of extreme poverty, trusting that God would fulfill His promise through the prophet. As a result, she experienced a miraculous provision,

> *"The bin of flour was not used up, nor did the jar of oil run dry, according to the word of the Lord"* (1 Kings 17:16).

Her sacrificial giving activated divine favor, leading to a supernatural provision that sustained her household throughout the famine.

This story demonstrates that God's favor is released in extraordinary ways when we give sacrificially, especially in times of lack or need. The widow's willingness to trust God and give what little she had opened the door to an ongoing supply of provision.

The Sacrifice Of Solomon: Activating Favor Through Worship

King Solomon is another powerful example of how sacrificial giving activates favor. After Solomon became king, he made a significant offering to God as an act of worship and gratitude. In 1 Kings 3:4, we read that Solomon went to Gibeon to offer sacrifices and offered *"a thousand burnt offerings on that altar."*

The law did not require this sacrificial offering, but Solomon chose to give extravagantly to honor God. His sacrifice caught God's attention, and that night, God appeared to Solomon in a dream and said, *"Ask! What shall I give you?"* (1 Kings 3:5). Solomon asked for wisdom to govern the people. Because of his selfless request, God granted him knowledge, wealth, honor, and long life (1 Kings 3:12-13).

Solomon's sacrificial giving activated a level of favor that transformed his entire reign. He became the wisest and wealthiest king in Israel's history, and his kingdom experienced peace and prosperity. This story illustrates that sacrificial giving, mainly when motivated by worship and gratitude, leads to an overflow of divine favor.

Mary's Alabaster Jar: A Gift Of Extravagant Love

Another powerful example of sacrificial giving is the story of Mary of Bethany, who anointed Jesus with expensive perfume shortly before His crucifixion. In (Matthew 26:6-13), we read that Mary broke an alabaster jar of costly perfume and poured it on Jesus' head as an act of worship and love. This perfume was worth a year's wages, making it an extravagant and sacrificial gift.

Some of the disciples criticized Mary, saying that the perfume could have been sold and the money given to people experiencing poverty. However, Jesus defended her, saying,

> *"Why do you trouble the woman? For she has done a good work for Me. … Assuredly, I say to you, wherever this gospel is preached in the whole world, what this woman has done will also be told as a memorial to her"* (Matthew 26:10, 13).

Mary's sacrificial giving expressed her deep love and devotion to Jesus. Her gift, though costly, demonstrated her faith and recognition of Jesus' worth. As a result, her act of worship was immortalized in Scripture, and she received divine favor in the form of honor and recognition throughout history.

This story teaches us that sacrificial giving has a lasting impact, especially out of love for God. It activates divine favor that goes beyond the immediate circumstances and leaves a lasting legacy.

How Sacrificial Giving Activates Divine Favor

Sacrificial giving is not just a matter of material exchange but a spiritual principle that unlocks God's supernatural favor. When we give sacrificially, we align ourselves with God's nature, as He is a generous and giving God. This alignment allows divine favor to flow into our lives in various ways.

- **Sacrificial Giving Demonstrates Trust in God's Provision**

One reason sacrificial giving activates favor is that it demonstrates our trust in God as our provider. We declare that God will care for us when we give out of our need or when the gift requires a personal cost. This trust in God's provision pleases Him and attracts His favor.

In Malachi 3:10, God challenges His people to test Him in giving. He says,

> *"Bring all the tithes into the storehouse, that there may be food in My house, and try Me now in this, says the Lord of hosts if I will not open for you the windows of heaven and pour out for you such blessing that there will not be room enough to receive it."*

While this passage refers explicitly to tithing, the principle applies to all forms of sacrificial giving. When we give, we are invited to demonstrate His faithfulness by providing for us in ways that exceed our expectations. Sacrificial giving activates favor because it shows that we trust God's promise to supply all our needs according to His riches in glory (Philippians 4:19).

• Sacrificial Giving Aligns Us with God's Heart

God is a generous God, and sacrificial giving reflects His heart. John 3:16 reminds us of the greatest act of sacrificial giving,

> *"For God so loved the world that He gave His only begotten Son, that whoever believes in Him should not perish but have everlasting life."*

God's gift of His Son was the ultimate sacrifice out of love for humanity. When we give sacrificially, we align ourselves with God's nature and participate in His work of love and redemption.

This alignment with God's heart attracts His favor. In 2 Corinthians 9:7, Paul writes,

> *"God loves a cheerful giver."*

When we give sacrificially and cheerfully, we reflect God's character, pleasing Him. As we offer in a way that mirrors God's generosity, we activate His favor in our lives.

• Sacrificial Giving Breaks the Power of Selfishness

Sacrificial giving also can break the hold of selfishness and materialism in our lives. When we give sacrificially, we declare that our trust is not in our possessions but in God's. This surrender allows God's favor to flow freely because it removes the obstacles of greed and selfishness that can block blessings.

Jesus taught in Matthew 6:24,

> *"No one can serve two masters; for either he will hate the one and love the other, or else he will be loyal to the one and despise the other. You cannot serve God and mammon."*

Sacrificial giving breaks the power of mammon (the spirit of materialism) and reaffirms that our allegiance is to God. When prioritizing God over material wealth, we position ourselves to receive His favor.

Practical Steps For Developing A Lifestyle Of Sacrificial Giving

Sacrificial giving is not something that happens only once in a lifetime; it is a lifestyle we can develop through intentional practice. Here are some practical steps for creating a heart of sacrificial giving that activates divine favor.

• Begin with a Willing Heart

Sacrificial giving starts with a heart willing to give, no matter the cost. In 2 Corinthians 8:12, Paul writes,

"For if there is first a willing mind, it is accepted according to what one has, and not according to what he does not have."

The key to sacrificial giving is not the amount but the willingness to give whatever God places on your heart. Ask God to help you develop a heart open to sharing, even when it is difficult.

• Pray for Opportunities to Give

One of the best ways to develop a lifestyle of sacrificial giving is to pray for opportunities to give. Ask God to show you where He wants you to sow and whom He wants you to bless. As you remain open and sensitive to the Holy Spirit's leading, God will provide opportunities for you to give sacrificially and activate His favor.

• Give Beyond Your Comfort Zone

Sacrificial giving requires stepping out of your comfort zone. This may involve giving more than you initially planned or giving in ways that stretch your faith. When you give beyond what is comfortable, you position yourself to experience God's miraculous provision and favor. Remember the widow of Zarephath, who gave her last meal to Elijah, and how God multiplied her resources in response to her sacrifice.

• Trust God for Provision

Finally, sacrificial giving requires trusting God to provide for your needs. When you give sacrificially, you make room for God to move supernaturally in your life. Philippians 4:19 promises,

> *"And my God shall supply all your need according to His riches in glory by Christ Jesus."*

As you trust God and give generously, He will pour out His favor in ways that exceed your expectations.

Finally, by developing a heart of sacrificial giving, we align ourselves with God's nature, break the hold of materialism, and position ourselves to receive His abundant favor. As we give cheerfully and generously, we can trust that God will open the windows of heaven and pour out blessings that we cannot contain.

CHAPTER ELEVEN

OBEDIENCE

◆ ◆ ◆

The Key To Sustaining Favor

The Blessings Of Obedience

Obedience to God's commands is the cornerstone of sustaining divine favor in every area of our lives. The Bible consistently links obedience with blessings, promising that those who walk in obedience will experience God's favor in abundance. In Deuteronomy 28:1-2, God sets forth a powerful promise to His people,

> *"Now it shall come to pass, if you diligently obey the voice of the Lord your God, to observe all His commandments which I command you today, that the Lord your God will set you high above all nations of the earth. And all these blessings shall come upon you and overtake you because you obey the voice of the Lord your God."*

Obedience Opens The Door To Blessings

The blessings of obedience are holistic, touching every aspect of our lives spiritually, financially, physically, and relationally. Obedience positions us to receive the full measure of God's promises, aligning us with His will and purpose.

- **Spiritual Blessings**: When we walk in obedience, we become intimate with God. Jesus said in John 14:23,

"If anyone loves Me, he will keep My word; and My Father will love him, and We will come to him and make Our home with him."

Obedience deepens our relationship with God and allows us to experience His presence fully. We draw closer to God through obedience, and His favor rests upon us.

- **Financial Blessings**: Obedience to God's principles concerning stewardship, giving, and generosity leads to financial favor. Malachi 3:10-12 connects tithing and financial obedience with blessings, saying,

"Bring all the tithes into the storehouse, that there may be food in My house, and try Me now in this, says the Lord of hosts if I will not open for you the windows of heaven and pour out for you such blessing that there will not be room enough to receive it."

Obedience in this area brings financial overflow and divine provision.

- **Physical Blessings:** The Bible also promises health and well-being due to obedience. Proverbs 3:7-8 says,

"Do not be wise in your own eyes; fear the Lord and depart from evil. It will be health to your flesh and strength to your bones."

Obedience to God's commands leads to physical health and vitality as we follow His wisdom in living and caring for our bodies.

- **Relational Blessings:** Obedience ensures favor in our relationships with others. We build solid and healthy relationships by obeying God's instructions to love, forgive, and serve one another. Ephesians 6:2-3 connects obedience to relational blessings when it says,

"Honor your father and mother,"

which is the first commandment with a promise, "that it may be well with you and you may live long on the earth." Honoring others through obedience results in relational peace and harmony.

Obedience Sustains And Multiplies Favor

While obedience opens the door to favor, it also sustains and multiplies favor over time. God is not just concerned with giving us temporary blessings; He desires that we walk in sustained favor throughout our lives. Sustaining favor requires ongoing obedience, as it aligns us with God's plans.

In the parable of the Talents (Matthew 25:14-30), Jesus teaches that faithful stewardship and obedience lead to increased blessings. The servant who obeyed his master by investing his talents was rewarded with even more. This parable illustrates that obedience is not just about receiving initial favor but about maintaining and growing in favor through faithful, ongoing obedience.

Biblical Examples Of Obedience And Favor

The Bible provides numerous examples of individuals who experienced extraordinary favor due to their obedience. These stories demonstrate that obedience is the pathway to sustained and multiplied favor, as God rewards those who diligently follow

His commands.

• Abraham: Obedience through Sacrifice

One of the most perfect examples of obedience leading to favor is found in the life of Abraham. God called Abraham to leave his homeland and go to a place He would show him, promising to make him a great nation. Genesis 12:1-2 records this call,

> *"Now the Lord had said to Abram: 'Get out of your country, from your family and your father's house to a land that I will show you. I will make you a great nation; I will bless you and make your name great; and you shall be a blessing."*

Abraham obeyed God without hesitation, leaving behind everything familiar to follow God's direction. This obedience activated divine favor in Abraham's life, as God blessed him with land, wealth, and descendants. But Abraham's most significant test of obedience came when God asked him to sacrifice his only son, Isaac. Despite the emotional and spiritual difficulty of this request, Abraham obeyed.

In Genesis 22:16-18, we see God's response to Abraham's obedience,

> *"By Myself, I have sworn, says the Lord, because you have done this thing, and have not withheld your son, your only son, blessing I will bless you, and multiplying I will multiply your descendants as the stars of the heaven and as the sand which is on the seashore."*

Abraham's obedience not only brought favor in his lifetime but secured transgenerational favor for his descendants.

• Joshua: Obedience in Battle

The story of Joshua and the battle of Jericho is another powerful example of obedience that results in favor. God gave Joshua specific instructions for conquering the city of Jericho, commanding him to have the people march around the city once a day for six days and seven times on the seventh day. This strategy likely seemed unconventional, but Joshua obeyed without question.

Joshua 6:2-5 records God's instructions, and verses 20-21 describe the outcome,

> *"So the people shouted when the priests blew the trumpets. And it happened, when the people heard the trumpet sound, and the people shouted with a great shout, that the wall fell flat."*

Joshua's obedience led to a miraculous victory, as God poured favor on Israel.

Joshua's story reminds us that obedience often requires us to trust God's ways, even when they do not make sense from a human perspective. But when we obey, we position ourselves for supernatural favor and breakthrough.

- **Mary, the Mother of Jesus: Obedience through Surrender**

Mary, the mother of Jesus, is another remarkable example of obedience leading to favor. When the angel Gabriel appeared to Mary, telling her that she would conceive and bear the Son of God, Mary responded with faith and obedience, saying,

> *"Behold the maidservant of the Lord! Let it be to me according to your word"* (Luke 1:38).

Despite the potential social stigma and personal sacrifice, Mary's willingness to obey God's plan led to her receiving unparalleled favor. In Luke 1:30, the angel told her,

"Do not be afraid, Mary, for you have found favor with God."

Her obedience resulted in her becoming the mother of the Messiah, a role that brought eternal significance and honor.

The Cost Of Disobedience

Just as obedience brings favor, disobedience can block favor and lead to negative consequences. The Bible warns us that disobedience leads to a loss of blessings and even judgment. When we choose to go our way instead of following God's instructions, we forfeit the favor that comes from walking in alignment with His will.

• Jonah: Disobedience and Divine Correction

Jonah is another example of how disobedience can lead to severe consequences. God commanded Jonah to go to Nineveh and preach against its wickedness. However, instead of obeying God's command, Jonah fled in the opposite direction, boarding a ship bound for Tarshish. Jonah's decision to disobey was motivated by his dislike for the Ninevites and his desire to avoid the difficult task of preaching to a people he believed were beyond redemption.

As a result of his disobedience, Jonah faced a series of dire consequences. A great storm arose while he was on the ship, threatening to sink it. The sailors, fearing for their lives, cast lots to determine who was responsible for the calamity, and the lot fell on Jonah. Realizing that his disobedience had put the crew in danger, Jonah confessed that he was the cause of the storm and instructed the sailors to throw him overboard.

In Jonah 1:12-15, we read,

> *"And he said to them, 'Pick me up and throw me into the sea; then the sea will become calm for you, for I know that this great tempest is because of me.' Nevertheless, the men rowed hard to return to land but could not, for the sea continued to grow more tempestuous against them, Therefore, they cried out to the Lord and said, 'We pray, O Lord, please do not let us perish for this man's life, and do not charge us with innocent blood; for You, O Lord, have done as it pleased You.' So they picked up Jonah and threw him into the sea, and the sea ceased from its raging."*

This act of being thrown into the sea led to Jonah being swallowed by a great fish, where he spent three days and nights. While in the belly of the fish, Jonah prayed and repented for his disobedience. He recognized that his choices had led him to a place of desperation and that he needed God's mercy.

In Jonah 2:1-2, he cried out,

> *"Then Jonah prayed to the Lord his God from the fish's belly. And he said: 'I cried out to the Lord because of my affliction, and He answered me."*

Jonah's prayer of repentance activated God's favor once again. After three days, God commanded the fish to vomit Jonah onto dry land, giving him a second chance to obey.

Jonah's story teaches us several important lessons about disobedience:

- **Disobedience Can Lead to Personal Crisis**: Jonah's decision to disobey God resulted in dire consequences for himself and the sailors on the ship. His actions highlight that our disobedience can impact those around us.

- **God's Mercy in Our Disobedience**: Despite Jonah's rebellion, God extended mercy when Jonah repented. God is always willing to forgive and restore us when we return to Him, no matter how far we've strayed.

- **Obedience Brings Restoration and Favor**: After Jonah repented, God commanded him to return to Nineveh. This time, Jonah obeyed and proclaimed God's message to the city. As a result, the people of Nineveh repented, and God spared them from destruction.

- **The Power of Obedience to Impact Others**: Jonah's eventual obedience led to a massive revival in Nineveh, demonstrating that our obedience can have far-reaching effects, bringing others to repentance and faith.

The Cost Of Disobedience In Our Lives

Disobedience can lead to various consequences in our lives, which can include:

- **Loss of Favor**: Just as Saul lost favor with God and man due to his disobedience, we, too, can forfeit favor when we choose our way instead of following God's commands. This loss of favor can impact our relationships, opportunities, and spiritual growth.

- **Personal Struggles and Trials**: Disobedience often leads to struggles and trials. When we step outside of God's will, we may encounter challenges that could have been avoided had we chosen to obey. The storms of life can arise as a result of our decisions, leading to unnecessary hardships.

- **Emotional and Spiritual Distress**: Disobedience can result in emotional and spiritual turmoil. When we know we are not walking in alignment with God's will, it can create a sense of guilt, shame, and distance from God. This emotional distress can hinder our ability to experience God's peace and joy.

- **Missed Opportunities:** God often has specific plans and purposes for our lives. We may miss out on the opportunities He has prepared for us when we disobey. Our disobedience can lead us down paths not aligned with His will, causing us to miss out on the blessings He desires to give us.

The Path To Restoration

While disobedience carries consequences, the path to restoration is always available through repentance and a return to obedience. The Bible contains stories of individuals who returned to God after straying from His ways. For example, King David, despite his grave sin of adultery and murder, repented wholeheartedly and received God's forgiveness.

Psalm 51 is a powerful prayer of repentance that reflects David's heart. In verse 10, he cries,

"Create in me a clean heart, O God, and renew a steadfast spirit within me."

David's desire for restoration and obedience opened the door for God's favor to be renewed.

Returning to God and seeking His mercy allows us to experience His grace and favor again. When we genuinely repent and turn away from disobedience, we can trust that God will restore us and bring us back into right standing with Him.

Living A Life Of Obedience

To sustain favor in our lives, we must commit to obedience. This involves daily choices that reflect our commitment to God's ways and His word.

Daily Choices Of Obedience

Obedience is often demonstrated in the small, everyday choices we make. Colossians 3:23-24 encourages us to "work heartily as for the Lord, not for men, knowing that you will receive the inheritance as a reward." This principle applies to our jobs, relationships, and responsibilities. When we act with integrity, diligence, and love, we live in obedience and position ourselves for favor.

For example, being honest in our business dealings, treating others with respect, and serving those in need are all ways to demonstrate obedience in our daily lives. These choices may seem small, but they reflect a heart that desires to please God and attract His favor.

The Role Of The Holy Spirit In Obedience

The Holy Spirit empowers us to live in obedience. Jesus promised that the Holy Spirit would guide us into all truth (John 16:13). When we yield to the Holy Spirit's leading, we receive the strength and wisdom to make decisions that align with God's will.

In Galatians 5:16, Paul instructs us to

> "walk in the Spirit, and you shall not fulfill the lust of the flesh."

Walking in the Spirit means relying on His guidance and strength to live a life of obedience. As we cultivate our relationship with the Holy Spirit, we become more attuned to His leading, making it easier to obey God's commands.

The Importance Of Accountability

Maintaining a lifestyle of obedience also involves surrounding ourselves with a community of believers who can encourage and hold us accountable. Hebrews 10:24-25 encourages us to

"consider one another to stir up love and good works, not forsaking the assembling of ourselves together."

Being part of a supportive Christian community helps us stay focused on obedience and encourages us to persevere.

Accountability can take many forms, including small groups, mentorship, or spiritual friendships. Sharing our struggles, successes, and prayer requests with others fosters an environment of growth and obedience. This community can help us stay committed to living righteously and experiencing God's favor.

The Fruit Of Obedience: Sustained Favor

The ultimate goal of obedience is to bear fruit that reflects God's glory. Jesus taught that obedience to His commands leads to a fruitful life. In John 15:5, He says, *"I am the vine, you are the branches. He who abides in Me, and I in him, bears much fruit; for without Me, you can do nothing."*

The Evidence Of Favor In Our Lives

When we walk in obedience, we can expect to see the evidence of God's favor manifesting in our lives. This may include:

- **Increased Wisdom**: (James 1:5) tells us that if we lack wisdom, we can ask God, who gives generously. As we obey, we grow in understanding and discernment, enabling us to navigate life's challenges effectively.

- **Divine Connections**: Obedience often leads to opportunities for connection with people who can help us fulfill our purpose. When we align ourselves with God's will, He places divine connections in our path that align with His plans.

- **Peace and Joy**: Walking in obedience brings peace and joy that surpasses circumstances. Philippians 4:7 promises,

"And the peace of God, which surpasses all understanding, will guard your hearts and minds through Christ Jesus."

This peace directly results from living in alignment with God's will.

- **Fruitful Relationships**: Obedience ensures healthy relationships with love, respect, and unity. We cultivate relationships that reflect His character as we treat others according to God's principles.

The Challenge Of Sustaining Obedience

While obedience attracts and sustains favor, it is essential to acknowledge that living a life of obedience can be challenging. The world often promotes values contradicting God's principles, making it easy to compromise our convictions.

- **The Pressure to Conform**: As believers, we face societal pressures that encourage compromise. (Romans 12:2) admonishes us not to be conformed to this world but to be transformed by renewing our minds. To sustain obedience, we must consciously reject worldly influences and align our thoughts with God's Word.

- **The Struggle Against the Flesh**: Obedience often requires overcoming our fleshly desires. Galatians 5:17 explains that

"the flesh lusts against the Spirit and the Spirit against the flesh, and these are contrary to one another."

We must continually choose to walk in the Spirit and resist the temptations that lead us away from obedience.

- **Maintaining Focus on God's Promises**: To sustain obedience, we must keep our eyes fixed on God's promises and the rewards of following Him. (Hebrews 12:1-2) encourages us to run with endurance the race set before us, looking unto Jesus, the author and finisher of our faith. When we focus on Jesus and His promises, we find the strength to remain obedient.

Lastly, obedience is the key to sustaining favor in our lives. It is not merely about following rules but cultivating a heart that desires to please God. The blessings of obedience are abundant, touching every area of our lives spiritually, financially, physically, and relationally.

Following the examples of biblical figures like Abraham, Joshua, and Mary, we can see that obedience leads to favor that lasts beyond our lifetime. As we commit to a lifestyle of obedience, seek the guidance of the Holy Spirit, develop accountability, and remain focused on God's promises, we can experience the fullness of His favor and bear fruit that glorifies Him.

CHAPTER TWELVE

WALKING IN FAVOR WITH GOD AND MAN

◆ ◆ ◆

The Dual Nature of Favor

F avor is a gift from God that extends beyond our relationship with Him and encompasses our relationships with others. Walking in favor with God and man means we experience divine blessings and favor in our spiritual lives while cultivating positive, godly relationships in the world around us. This dual nature of favor is essential for fulfilling God's purpose in our lives and impacting others.

Understanding Favor With God

Favor with God is primarily about our relationship with Him. It is rooted in our obedience, faith, and love for Him. Walking closely with Him, we experience His presence, guidance, and blessings. This favor is not earned through good works but results from our faith in Christ and our commitment to living according to God's Word.

In Luke 2:52,

"Jesus increased in wisdom and stature, and in favor with God and men."

This verse highlights the importance of both dimensions of favor in Jesus's life. His relationship with God was characterized by obedience and love, which led to divine favor. As followers of Christ, we are called to emulate His example.

The Importance Of Favor With Man

While favor with God is paramount, favor with man is also essential for fulfilling God's plan. Favor with others opens doors to opportunities, relationships, and resources that can further our mission and purpose. God often uses people to bless us, and maintaining good relationships is vital to experiencing favor in our lives.

In Proverbs 3:3-4, we are encouraged to

"let not mercy and truth forsake you; bind them around your neck, write them on the tablet of your heart, and so find favor and high esteem in the sight of God and man."

This passage highlights that mercy and truth are vital attributes that lead to favor in our relationships with others. When we embody these qualities, we create an environment where favor can flourish.

Biblical Examples Of Favor With God And Man

The Bible provides several examples of individuals who experienced favor with God and man, demonstrating how these two dimensions of favor work together.

• Joseph: A Life of Favor

Joseph's life is a remarkable example of how favor with God and man can manifest simultaneously. After his brothers sold him into slavery, Joseph was taken to Egypt, where he served in the household of Potiphar. Despite his difficult circumstances, Joseph remained faithful and walked with integrity, which resulted in God's favor resting upon him. Genesis 39:2-3 says,

> *"The Lord was with Joseph, and he was a successful man, and he was in the house of his master the Egyptian. And his master saw that the Lord was with him and made all he did prosper in his hand."*

This favor with God led to favor with Potiphar, who recognized Joseph's exceptional qualities and promoted him to oversee his household.

However, Joseph faced a significant trial when he was falsely accused by Potiphar's wife and thrown into prison. Even in prison, God's favor was with Joseph, as we see in Genesis 39:21,

> *"But the Lord was with Joseph and showed him mercy, and He gave him favor in the sight of the keeper of the prison."*

Joseph's unwavering faith and integrity led to favor with the prison keeper, who entrusted him with responsibilities.

Eventually, Joseph's ability to interpret dreams brought him before Pharaoh, where he interpreted the dreams that foretold a coming famine. Pharaoh recognized Joseph's wisdom and appointed him as second-in-command over Egypt, stating,

> *"Since God has shown you all this, there is no one as*

discerning and wise as you" (Genesis 41:39).

is a profound example of how Joseph's favor with God resulted in favor with Pharaoh and positioned him to fulfill God's purpose for his life.

• Esther: A Woman of Favor

The story of Esther illustrates the power of favor with both God and man. Esther was a Jewish woman who became queen of Persia when her people were threatened by destruction. When Mordecai, her cousin, urged her to approach the king and plead for her people, Esther demonstrated remarkable courage and obedience.

Before approaching the king, Esther fasted and prayed, seeking God's guidance and favor (Esther 4:16). Her commitment to prayer and seeking God positioned her to act wisely when the moment came. When she entered the king's presence, she found favor in his sight as the king extended his scepter to her (Esther 5:2).

Esther's favor with the king allowed her to host a banquet where she revealed her Jewish identity and the plot against her people. As a result of her boldness and reliance on God, the king issued a decree that saved the Jewish people from destruction. Esther's life exemplifies how favor with God, cultivated through prayer and obedience, can lead to favor with influential individuals, allowing us to fulfill our divine assignments.

• Daniel: A Model of Integrity and Favor

The life of Daniel further exemplifies the importance of walking in favor of God and man. Daniel was taken captive to Babylon, where he maintained his faith and commitment to God despite the pressures to conform to the Babylonian culture. Daniel 1:8 says,

"But Daniel purposed in his heart that he would not defile himself with the portion of the king's delicacies, nor with the wine which he drank."

Daniel's obedience to God's dietary laws led to favor with the chief eunuch, who allowed him to eat vegetables and water instead of the king's rich food (Daniel 1:12-13). God's favor was evident as Daniel and his friends appeared healthier and better nourished than those who ate the king's food.

Daniel's continued faithfulness and integrity attracted favor in every area of his life. He rose to leadership positions within the Babylonian kingdom, eventually becoming the chief governor over all the wise men of Babylon. His ability to interpret dreams and visions, a God-given gift, further enhanced his favor with the king.

In Daniel 6:3, it is noted,

"Then this Daniel distinguished himself above the governors and satraps because an excellent spirit was in him, and the king gave thought to set him over the whole realm."

Daniel's unwavering faith, integrity, and excellence resulted in a favorable outcome that impacted his life and those around him.

Cultivating Favor In Our Relationships

While favor with God is essential, cultivating favor with others is equally important. Our relationships with family, friends, colleagues, and community members significantly influence how favor is experienced and expressed.

The Importance Of Relationship Building

Favor is often cultivated through the relationships we build. Proverbs 18:24 says,

"A man with friends must be friendly."

Building healthy, godly relationships requires effort and intentionality. When we invest time and care into our relationships, we create an environment where favor can flourish.

Favor with others can lead to collaboration, support, and encouragement opportunities. Developing genuine connections enriches our lives and positions us to experience God's favor through others. Building relationships based on trust, respect, and mutual support is essential for sustaining favor over time.

The Role Of Humility In Relationships

Humility is a critical component of cultivating favor in relationships. James 4:6 reminds us, *"God resists the proud but gives grace to the humble."* Humility opens the door for favor because it creates an atmosphere of respect and honor in our interactions with others.

When we approach relationships humbly, we demonstrate a willingness to listen, serve, and support others. Humility fosters an environment where favor can flow freely, as others are drawn to our genuine character. We create a foundation for lasting relationships that attract favor by valuing and respecting those around us.

- **Practicing Kindness and Generosity**

Practicing kindness and generosity is another way to cultivate favor in our relationships. Acts of kindness, whether small or large, demonstrate love and care for others. Proverbs 11:25 says,

> *"The generous soul will be made rich, and he who waters will also be watered himself."*

When we extend kindness and generosity to others, we create a cycle of favor that benefits everyone involved.

Being generous with our time, resources, and talents positions us to receive favor from others. For example, volunteering in our communities, helping a neighbor, or supporting a friend in need are all ways to demonstrate kindness that can lead to positive relationships and favor.

· **The Power of Forgiveness**

Forgiveness is essential for maintaining healthy relationships and cultivating favor. Holding onto grudges or resentment can create barriers that block favor from flowing in our lives. Ephesians 4:32 encourages us to

> *"be kind to one another, tenderhearted, forgiving one another, even as God in Christ forgave you."*

Forgiving others releases us from bitterness and opens the door for healing and reconciliation. When we practice forgiveness, we create an environment where favor can thrive. Others are drawn to our character, and our relationships are strengthened.

The Role Of Wisdom In Walking In Favour

Wisdom is crucial for walking in favor of both God and man. The Bible repeatedly emphasizes the importance of wisdom in our relationships and decision-making.

Seeking Godly Wisdom

Proverbs 4:7 says,

> *"Wisdom is the principal thing; therefore, get wisdom.*
> *And in all, you're getting, get understanding."*

Seeking godly wisdom in our relationships helps us navigate challenges and make decisions that align with God's will. When we approach situations with wisdom, we are better equipped to foster favor with others.

Praying for wisdom is essential. James 1:5 encourages us,

> *"If any of you lacks wisdom, let him ask of God, who gives*
> *to all liberally and without reproach, and it will be given*
> *to him."*

By seeking God's wisdom in prayer, we invite His guidance into our relationships and decision-making processes.

The Fruit Of Wisdom In Relationships

Wisdom produces fruit in our relationships. When we apply God's wisdom in our interactions, we cultivate love, patience, and understanding. Proverbs 16:21 says,

> *"The wise in heart will be called prudent, and sweetness*
> *of the lips increases learning."*

Wise words and actions lead to better communication and

stronger bonds with those around us.

For instance, applying wisdom can help us respond with grace and clarity when faced with conflicts or misunderstandings. Instead of reacting impulsively, we can listen, empathize, and find common ground. This approach fosters favor and strengthens relationships, as people appreciate our thoughtful and considerate responses.

Walking In Integrity

Integrity is a vital aspect of walking in favor of God and man. It involves honesty, trustworthiness, and consistency in our actions and words. Proverbs 10:9 states,

> *"He who walks with integrity walks securely, but he who perverts his ways will become known."*

When we live with integrity, we create a foundation of trust that attracts favor from others.

Integrity involves making choices that align with our values, even when difficult. When we demonstrate integrity in our personal and professional lives, we earn the respect and admiration of those around us. People are more likely to extend favor to individuals they trust and respect.

The Overflow Of Favour

Walking in favor with both God and man leads to an overflow of blessings in our lives. As we experience God's favor, we are empowered to bless others, creating a ripple effect of favor beyond ourselves.

- **Being a Blessing to Others**

As recipients of God's favor, we can bless others. This is an essential aspect of walking in favor. When we actively seek ways to bless those around us, we position ourselves to experience more excellent favor. The principle of sowing and reaping is evident in this context,

> "Give, and it will be given to you: good measure, pressed down, shaken together, and running over will be put into your bosom" (Luke 6:38).

Being a blessing can take many forms, offering encouragement, helping someone in need, or using our resources to support others. We create an environment where favor multiplies when we extend kindness and generosity.

· Encouraging Others in Their Walk with God

Walking in favor also means encouraging others in their relationship with God. When we share our testimonies of God's faithfulness and favor, we inspire others to trust Him and pursue His favor. Encouragement fosters community and support, helping us grow in our faith.

In 1 Thessalonians 5:11, Paul instructs us to

> "encourage one another and build each other up."

This principle applies not only to our relationships but also to our walk with God. When we uplift and encourage others, we contribute to a culture of favor that honors God.

The Legacy Of Favor

Walking in favor of God and man creates a legacy that impacts future generations. As we cultivate relationships based on flavor, integrity, and love, we leave behind a legacy others can follow. Proverbs 13:22 reminds us,

> *"A good man leaves an inheritance to his children's children."*

This inheritance is not merely material but includes the spiritual and relational favor we pass on.

As we model a life of favor, we inspire our children, friends, and community members to seek God and walk in His ways. The legacy of favor we leave can influence generations to come, creating a culture of obedience, kindness, and generosity.

Following the examples of biblical figures like Joseph, Esther, and Daniel, we learn that favor is a powerful gift that can change lives. By cultivating relationships based on love and trust, we open ourselves to the overflow of God's blessings.

Let us walk in favor with God and man, trusting that our obedience and relationships will lead to a life marked by God's goodness and favor. As we do, we will see the transformative power of favor manifest in our lives and those around us.

CHAPTER THIRTEEN

THE OVERFLOW OF FAVOR: BLESSING OTHERS

◆ ◆ ◆

Understanding the Overflow of Favor

The concept of overflow is significant in the Christian life, especially concerning God's favor. When discussing the overflow of favor, we refer to the abundance of blessings God pours into our lives, allowing us to bless others. This overflow is not meant to be contained within ourselves but should spill out into the lives of those around us.

In Psalm 23:5, David writes,

> "You prepare a table before me in the presence of my enemies; You anoint my head with oil; my cup runs over."

This imagery of an overflowing cup signifies abundance and blessing. God's favor is so profound that it meets our needs and provides us with excess to share with others.

When we experience the overflow of favor, we must recognize our responsibility to share these blessings with those in need. This principle is deeply rooted in Scripture, where we are called conduits of God's love and generosity in the world.

The Biblical Foundation For Blessing Others

The call to bless others is a recurring theme throughout the Bible. From the Old Testament to the New Testament, we see God's intention for His people to be a source of blessing to the nations.

- **God's Covenant with Abraham**: In Genesis 12:2-3, God promises Abraham,

"I will make you a great nation; I will bless you and make your name great; and you shall be a blessing. I will bless those who bless you, and I will curse him who curses you, and in you, all the families of the earth shall be blessed."

God's covenant with Abraham was not just for his benefit; it was intended to extend to all the families of the earth. Abraham's obedience to God resulted in a legacy of blessing that continues to impact the world today.

- **The Law of Moses**: The Mosaic Law included various instructions for how the Israelites cared for people experiencing poverty, widows, and orphans. In Deuteronomy 15:7-8, God commands,

"If there is among you a poor man of your brethren, within any of the gates in your land which the Lord your God is giving you, you shall not harden your heart nor shut your hand from your poor brother, but you shall open your hand wide to him and willingly lend him enough for his need,

whatever he needs."

These instructions demonstrate God's heart for the vulnerable and His desire for His people to be generous and compassionate.

- **The Teachings of Jesus**: Jesus continued blessing others throughout His ministry. In Matthew 25:35-40, Jesus identifies Himself with the marginalized, saying, *"For I was hungry, and you gave Me food; I was thirsty, and you gave Me drink; I was a stranger, and you took Me in; I was naked, and you clothed Me; I was sick, and you visited Me; I was in prison, and you came to Me."*

Jesus teaches that our acts of kindness and generosity towards others are ultimately acts of service to Him.

- **The Early Church**: The early church exemplified the overflow of favor in their community. Acts 2:44-45 states,

"Now all who believed were together, and had all things in common, and sold their possessions and goods, and divided them among all, as anyone had need."

The believers shared their resources, ensuring that no one lacked anything. This spirit of generosity directly resulted from experiencing God's favor and grace.

The Call To Generosity

We are called to reflect His generosity as recipients of God's favor. The Bible repeatedly emphasizes the importance of generosity and its connection to the overflow of favor.

- **The Principle of Sowing and Reaping**: In 2 Corinthians 9:6-8, Paul writes,

"But this I say: He who sows sparingly will also reap sparingly, and he who sows bountifully will also reap bountifully. So let each one give as he purposes in his heart, not grudgingly or of necessity, for God loves a cheerful giver. And God can make all grace abound toward you, that you, always having all sufficiency in all things, may have an abundance for every good work."

This principle teaches us that generosity activates God's favor and provision in our lives.

- **The Heart of Giving**: God desires that we give not out of obligation but love and gratitude, the heart behind our giving matters. When we give joyfully and willingly, we position ourselves to experience the overflow of God's blessings. Our generosity reflects the character of God, who is the ultimate giver.

- **Blessing Others as an Act of Worship**: Giving should be seen as worship and gratitude towards God. In Philippians 4:18, Paul describes the gifts he received from the Philippians as

"a sweet-smelling aroma, an acceptable sacrifice, well pleasing to God."

Our acts of generosity are a form of worship that pleases God and invites His favor.

The Spiritual Significance Of Blessing Others.

Blessing others goes beyond meeting physical needs; it has profound spiritual significance. When we bless others, we reflect God's love and character, demonstrating His grace and mercy in tangible ways.

- **Building Community and Connection**: Blessing others fosters community and connection. When we extend kindness and generosity, we strengthen our relationships and create a supportive network of believers. This community is a reflection of the body of Christ, where each member contributes to the well-being of others.

- **Encouraging Spiritual Growth**: When we bless others, we create opportunities for spiritual growth for ourselves and those we serve. Acts of kindness and generosity often lead to conversations about faith and hope. As we share God's love through our actions, we encourage others to seek a deeper relationship.

- **Demonstrating God's Kingdom**: Our acts of blessing reflect the values of God's Kingdom. In Matthew 5:16, Jesus instructs us to "let your light so shine before men, that they may see your good works and glorify your Father in heaven." When we live out our faith through acts of kindness and generosity, we showcase the transformative power of God's love to the world around us.

- **Fulfilling the Great Commission**: The call to bless others aligns with the Great Commission. Jesus commanded us to go and make disciples of all nations (Matthew 28:19-20). As we bless others, we create opportunities to share the Gospel and invite them into a relationship with Christ. Our acts of kindness can serve as a bridge to share the good news of salvation.

Practical Ways To Bless Others

As we understand the importance of blessing others and the overflow of God's favor, we must explore practical ways to do this daily. Here are some ways to actively engage in blessing others:

- **Acts of Kindness**

Simple acts of kindness can have a significant impact on those around us. These small gestures such as offering a smile, holding the door open for someone, or complimenting a friend, create positivity and goodwill.

- **Random Acts of Kindness:** Consider committing to random acts of kindness each week. This could include buying a coffee for the person in line behind you, leaving a generous tip for a server, or writing an encouraging note to a friend. These acts not only bless others but also create an atmosphere of generosity.

- **Support Local Initiatives**: Engage with local charities, food banks, or community organizations that serve those in need. Volunteering your time or resources can be a powerful way to bless others and make a difference in your community.

- **Sharing Resources:** God blesses us with resources for a reason, and sharing them is essential to blessing others.

- **Financial Support**: Consider supporting a missionary, a local charity, or a needy family. Your financial support can meet needs and empower others to continue working for God's kingdom.

- **Sharing Skills and Talents**: Use your unique

skills and talents to bless others. If you are a skilled carpenter, offer to help a neighbor with home repairs. If you are musically gifted, consider volunteering to lead worship at your church or perform at community events. Sharing our gifts is a way to reflect God's generosity and love.

Offering Time And Attention

In today's fast-paced world, giving our time and attention is one of our most precious gifts.

- **Deliberate Listening**: Take the time to listen to others genuinely. Give them your full attention when friends or family members share their struggles or joys. Your willingness to listen can be a blessing and demonstrate that you care.

- **Spending Quality Time**: Make an effort to spend quality time with loved ones, especially those who may be feeling lonely or isolated. Simple activities such as going for a walk, sharing a meal, or enjoying a game night can strengthen relationships and provide encouragement.

Praying For Others

Prayer is a powerful way to bless others and invite God's favor into their lives.

- **Intercessory Prayer**: Make it a habit to pray for others regularly. Keep a prayer journal with the names of those you wish to pray for and lift them before God. Interceding on behalf of others invites God's favor into their circumstances and demonstrates your love for them.

- **Offering to Pray with Others:** When someone shares a burden or need, offer to pray. This act not only blesses them but also fosters a deeper connection and encourages them to seek God's guidance and support.

Building A Culture Of Blessing

Creating a culture of blessing within our families, communities, and churches is essential for experiencing the overflow of favor.

Encouraging Generosity In Your Family

Start within your family by teaching and modeling generosity. Discuss the importance of giving and serving others, and involve your family in acts of kindness together. This could include volunteering at a local shelter, organizing a family donation drive, or hosting a meal for those in need.

Creating Family Traditions:
Consider establishing family traditions centered around giving and service. For example, focus on blessing others during holidays by donating to charity or volunteering together. These traditions instill the values of kindness and generosity in your children and create lasting memories.

Having a Generous Community
Encourage your church or community to embrace a culture of generosity and blessing. This can be done through organizing outreach events, mission trips, or service projects that allow members to engage with the needs of those around them.

Events:
Host events encouraging community involvement, such as food drives, clothing swaps, or free community meals. These gatherings meet practical needs, build relationships, and ensure

a sense of belonging.

Being a Model of Favor

As individuals who have experienced God's favor, we are called to be models of that favor in our interactions with others. Our lives should reflect the love and generosity that come from a relationship with Christ.

Living Authentically:

Let your actions speak louder than your words. When others see the love of Christ reflected in your life, they will be drawn to the message of hope and favor that you carry.

Testifying to God's Goodness:

Share your testimonies of God's favor with others. When you recount how God has blessed you, it encourages others to seek Him and believe in His ability to bless them.

Understanding The Ripple Effect Of Blessings

The overflow of favor creates a ripple effect that extends far beyond our immediate actions. When we bless others, we impact their lives and inspire them to pass on that blessing to others.

- **Creating a Chain Reaction**: Imagine a scenario where one act of kindness inspires someone to do something kind for another. This chain reaction can create a culture of generosity and compassion that transforms communities.

- **A Legacy of Generosity**: As we model a life of blessing and generosity, we leave behind a legacy that future generations can follow. Our children and those we influence will carry forward the principles of favor and generosity, continuing to bless others long after we are gone.

In conclusion, living in the overflow of God's favor involves actively seeking opportunities to bless others. As we experience God's blessings, we are called to reflect that generosity in our relationships, communities, and the world. We can cultivate a culture of blessing that impacts those around us through biblical principles, practical actions, and a heart of compassion. By recognizing our responsibility as recipients of favor, we can become conduits of God's love and grace, demonstrating His goodness to the world.

CONCLUSION

As we conclude this book, we are reminded that God's favor is a precious gift accessible to all who seek Him with a sincere heart. Throughout this book, we have examined various keys that unlock the door to divine favor and seen how these principles can transform our lives and impact those around us.

Understanding The Nature Of Favor

Favor is not merely a random act of kindness from God but a reflection of His love and grace toward us. It is about being positioned in a way that aligns us with God's will and purpose. When we embrace our identity as children of God, we begin to understand that we are heirs to His promises, and His favor is part of our inheritance.

The Role Of Obedience

One of the central themes of this book is the importance of obedience in sustaining favor. Biblical figures such as Abraham, Joseph, and Esther teach us that obedience is not just a duty; it is a pathway to experiencing God's blessings. When we walk in obedience, we open ourselves to His guidance, protection, and favor.

The Overflow Of Blessings

As we embody a lifestyle of favor, we also recognize the responsibility that comes with it. God's blessings are not meant to be hoarded; they are meant to overflow into the lives of others. When we bless those around us, we participate in God's plan to bring hope, healing, and transformation to our communities. The principle of sowing and reaping reminds us that the more we give, the more we receive, creating a cycle of generosity and favor.

Living In Community

Throughout this book, we emphasized the importance of building relationships and encouraging a culture of blessing within our families, churches, and communities. God designed us for connection, and when we actively seek to bless others, we reflect His character and purpose. Our acts of kindness, generosity, and encouragement can create a ripple effect that impacts countless lives.

The Lifelong Journey

Favor is not a destination; it is a lifelong journey. As we navigate the ups and downs of life, we can confidently approach each day, knowing that God's favor is available to us. This journey requires intentionality, faith, and perseverance. It calls us to remain anchored in God's Word, to seek His wisdom, and to trust in His plans.

The Invitation To Experience Favor

In the end, this book's message is an invitation to each reader to experience the fullness of God's favor. It is an invitation to embrace the keys that unlock His blessings, to walk in obedience, and to be a blessing to others. As we engage in this divine relationship with God, we will witness His favor manifest in ways that surpass our understanding.

In closing, let us remember the words of Psalm 90:17,

> *"And let the beauty of the Lord our God be upon us, and establish the work of our hands for us; yes, establish the work of our hands."*

May we continue to seek God's favor in all that we do, trusting that He will guide, bless, and use us to bring glory to His name.

Let us pray For the favor of God to be upon us as we embark on this journey.

Heavenly Father, we thank You for the gift of favor. We acknowledge that it is not something we earn but a blessing from You. Help us to walk in obedience to Your Word and to share the overflow of Your blessings with others. May Your favor rest upon us as we seek to fulfill your life purpose. Empower us to be vessels of Your love and grace, impacting those around us for Your glory. In Jesus' name, we pray. Amen.

ABOUT THE BOOK

"Golden Keys To Ultimate Favor" explores the profound principles that unlock divine favor. The book emphasizes the importance of obedience, sacrificial giving, and developing a generous heart through biblical teachings and examples. Readers will discover how favor reflects God's grace, offering spiritual, financial, and relational blessings.

The book encourages embracing a lifestyle of kindness and generosity, illustrating that the overflow of favor is meant to bless others and create a ripple effect in our communities. With practical steps for walking in favor of God and man, this book guides anyone seeking to deepen their relationship with God and experience His blessings. Finally, it invites readers to live in alignment with God's purpose, ensuring a legacy of favor that impacts their lives and those around them.

www.ingramcontent.com/pod-product-compliance
Lightning Source LLC
Chambersburg PA
CBHW071854020426
42331CB00010B/2516